life
is the curriculum

life
is the curriculum

Exploring the Foundations
of Care for Young Children
through the Insights of
Rudolf Steiner, Founder
of Waldorf Education

Cynthia Aldinger

Also by the author

Home Away from Home: LifeWays Care of Children and Families (with Mary O'Connell)

Acknowledgments

Without the profound research and insights of Rudolf Steiner, this book and the foundation of my work in early childhood would not exist. You are welcome to read about Dr. Steiner's research and my personal journey of discovery through his work in the section titled "About Rudolf Steiner."

It is also noteworthy that LifeWays would not be the healthy and strong organization it is without the devotion, care and enthusiasm of my amazing colleagues. It is wonderful to be able to say that there are really too many to name at this point in our development. The expansion of our opportunities to provide training and consulting to so many individuals, child care centers and homes, schools and families is due to the dedication of many teachers, student services directors, administrative support teams, and the indefatigable staff of LifeWays North America.

Another group of individuals that have deeply impacted our growing understanding of the needs of young children and families is our students across North America and beyond. It is a privilege to learn so much from those who come to learn from us.

Finally, there are a few people who must be mentioned by name since the very form and layout of this book would not have come to pass in such a beautiful presentation without them. Our book designer, Chelsea Cloeter, is easy to work with and has shown us once again that she has a fine eye for graphic detail and page design. Before the design stage, our proofreader, Ann Erwin, cleaned up my old-fashioned grammar and typing. (What happened to that second space after a period? I miss it so much!) Rahima Dancy was also active in the proofreading arena. As a successful author herself she, too, has kept up with the changes! Mary O'Connell, my dear co-author in *Home Away from Home*, kept things moving forward and also helped to select the beautiful photos. Renate Long-Breipohl offered a lovely foreword for which I am also very grateful.

My beloved grandchildren, to whom I dedicate this book, provided some of the stories I share regarding child development. I am blessed to visit them often enough to observe the wonder and joy of their delightful changes from newborns to first smiles to toe-sucking to becoming upright and walking to learning songs and games at their preschools. Very soon, I'll watch my first-born grandson go off to first grade! I would not have these sweet ones in my life were it not for their parents, our sons and daughters-in-law. Going back another generation, I have my dear husband, Michael, to thank for raising our children with me, and now playing such a lovely role as Financial Advisor to our students. If we go back even further, I am pleased to be able to acknowledge my parents who, at ninety-one and ninety-two, continue to be active, including taking care of babies and toddlers in their church nursery! I'm also grateful that my two sisters are always there for me.

It is hard to stop! Once we allow gratitude to swell up in our hearts, we start thinking of more and more people who have changed our lives significantly. I would like to mention one who helped to set me on my course as a teacher and educator. Georg Locher was my major professor at Emerson College in England, where I trained to become a Waldorf teacher. Though the slightly irreverent skits I created for our student events put a little worry in his soul as to whether I was really good material for early childhood, he very kindly gave me two thumbs up when he traveled to the States and observed me in my third year as a kindergarten teacher. We went on to briefly become colleagues at Antioch University when I was teaching in various trainings. He required of his students to stretch and grow and to be always mindful of the source of our inspiration. Bless you, dear Georg, on your light-filled journey through the heavens.

My humble and heartfelt thanks to all.

Cynthia Aldinger

Contents

FOREWORD　9

ABOUT RUDOLF STEINER　13

INTRODUCTION
What Do Young Children Need at Home and in Programs?　17

1. *Life as Curriculum*　23

2. *Child as Curriculum*　37

3. *Adult as Curriculum/Child as Apprentice*　53

4. *Environment as Curriculum*　75

IN CONCLUSION　91

APPENDICES
About LifeWays North America　93
Sources　95

Foreword

This most recent book by Cynthia Aldinger is a wonderful addition to her previous publications about early childhood care and education. *Life Is the Curriculum* includes Cynthia's own journey of discovery during her three decades of experience in Steiner education, making the book very inviting and accessible to readers with whatever background. No previous knowledge of Steiner Education is asked for, but a picture unfolds of a lifelong commitment to children and families and the quest to understand what is essential in caring for and educating the young child following the insights of Rudolf Steiner.

Through her previous experience as a Steiner/Waldorf kindergarten teacher, Cynthia realized that what is of benefit for a group of children aged 4–6 years is different from what is needed for a smaller, multi-aged group of children between birth and 6 years of age. That Steiner early childhood education can be done in such a different setting without compromising on the foundations and that working in a homelike environment has many benefits, especially for the young child of today, are just two of the things Cynthia has experienced in her own work and demonstrates to the wider public in this book.

But it is more than this. Even though the book is written in the style of a personal narration and reflection, what she has to say is clearly structured and builds upon the pedagogical foundations and four main pillars developed by LifeWays and called the *Living Arts:* Practical, Domestic Activity; Nurturing Care; Creative Exploration and Skill Development; and Social Awareness. The way in which Cynthia presents her ideas and experiences is unique. She has divided the book into four main areas of "curriculum": Life as Curriculum, Child as Curriculum, Adult as Curriculum, and Environment as Curriculum. The reader senses that the term "curriculum" is really insufficient to describe what the young child needs in order to grow into a healthy human being. Cynthia has consciously chosen this term because it is commonly used in educational planning and practice. However, what she describes and suggests goes far beyond the usual focus of curricula, such as acquiring intellectual, emotional/social, and physical abilities deemed necessary for a successful life in modern society. Her book is about creating a wholesome life around the child, in which the child is nurtured and can grow and develop at his or her own pace, protected from premature demands on intellectual and emotional-social faculties as is so common in today's culture. From her own knowledge and experience, she emphasizes that less is often more. Cynthia promotes the importance of slowing down in pace and avoiding sensory overload in children—in short, keeping life around the young child simple and real.

Throughout the book Cynthia refers to the spiritual-scientific research of Rudolf Steiner which became the foundation for her own work. She has included essential quotations from Steiner's educational lecture series in all four main chapters of the book and elaborates on how they look in practice. At times her reflections read like a commentary to these quotations, and bring them to life. At the end of each of the main chapters, Cynthia presents a set of questions related to the content of the chapter, inviting the reader to engage in a process of reflection. What a wonderful way of encouraging the step from passive to active reading! This makes the book very suitable not only for practicing early childhood teachers/caregivers and parents, but also for early childhood students.

I would like to draw attention especially to parts two and three, which lead the reader more deeply into the foundations of Steiner early childhood education through their themes, the child as curriculum and the adult as curriculum. Here, in the central part of the book, Cynthia has created the space to represent the spiritual foundations of working with young children. In the "Child as Curriculum" chapter she addresses the three phases of development in early childhood and ways to support the three essential developmental steps in becoming a human being: walking, talking and thinking. The development of these faculties is universal to all children.

Cynthia then continues: "The young child is both individual and universal from the very beginning. There are archetypal developmental milestones we come to expect in every typically developing child.... And if we are paying close attention, we may also notice subtle differences in how they move, what makes them feel soothed ... what sorts of sounds attract their attention and any number of other things." There follow considerations on ways to support the achievement of these three milestones of development, with reference to the research of Emmi Pikler and Sally Goddard Blythe. The chapter ends with practical advice on how to guide young children, an approach to discipline she calls *L.O.V.E.*. This abbreviation stands for listening, laughter, objectivity, order, versatility, vulnerability, energy and enthusiasm. "There are many tools available in each of these categories; however, the number-one tool is training oneself always to remember the spiritual nature of the young child."

In the "Adult as Curriculum/Child as Apprentice" chapter Cynthia writes about working with imitation and example—imitation being the main way in which a child learns. For the adult it means that being an example worthy to be imitated by children is a constant task and at times a great challenge. Much of what is described in part one as the *Living Arts* is now considered from the aspect of the self-development of the adult. Again, Cynthia has chosen to talk about this from the viewpoint of her own self-development as well as the general experience of challenges that await the educator on this path. "Rudolf Steiner offered us all a profound understanding of what it is to be an eternally unfolding being, cared for and in league with a multitude of other non-physical devoted Beings." Cynthia then points to some of the challenges involved in stretching beyond one's upbringing to concepts that are unfamiliar and yet make sense when one learns to observe young children with an open mind and heart. This part ends with considerations on relationship-based care, advocacy for children, environments suitable for young children and much more.

This is a book written with joy and enthusiasm for childhood and for the great and meaningful task of caring for the young: "Early childhood is that ripe and rosy time when, fresh from heaven's light, children arrive open and trusting that what we bring them will represent the goodness of the world. It is a time for long pauses, quiet and rowdy play, touching, tasting, smelling and rolling around in everything, and for experiencing striving adults who, while still growing up themselves, are eager to find some semblance of joy in life. It is a time to feel 'home' as a quality of experience as much as a place. It is a time for growing secure and safe and loved."

Renate Long-Breipohl
Author on Steiner Early Childhood Education and
Senior Lecturer at Sydney Rudolf Steiner College in Australia,
she advises and lectures around the world.

About Rudolf Steiner (1861–1925)

One can find many articles describing the life and times of Rudolf Steiner. The following is an excerpt from one of my favorite descriptions; it is posted on the website "Why Waldorf Works":

> Beginning at the end of the 19th century, a relatively unknown Austrian philosopher and teacher began to sow the seeds of what he hoped would blossom into a new culture. The seeds were his ideas, which he sowed through extensive writings, lectures and countless private consultations. The seeds germinated and took root in the hearts and minds of his students.... Since the teacher's death in 1925, a quiet but steadily growing movement, unknown and unseen by most people, has been spreading over the world, bringing practical solutions to the problems of our global, technological civilization. The seeds are now coming to flower in the form of thousands of projects infused with human values. The teacher, called by some "the best kept secret of the 20th century," was Rudolf Steiner. Over a period of forty years, he formulated and taught a path of inner development or spiritual research he called anthroposophy. From what he learned, he gave practical indications for nearly every field of human endeavor.
>
> —Christopher Bamford and Eric Utne

Although Rudolf Steiner was not alive when I was getting my formal education, he has become a lifelong teacher/mentor/advisor to me through the profound knowledge he shared during his lifetime. For many of us fortunate enough to have encountered this content, our lives have been forever changed. My story is just one of many examples.

At nineteen years old, I met my future husband, an interesting young man who told me stories of a much larger picture of life than I had ever heard. We both worked for the Zoology Department at the University of Oklahoma, and we would take long walks across campus under the guise of running errands. It seemed that, no matter what the subject, he had a more profound spin on it than what came up in conversations with my "normal" friends. Always he credited these ideals to Rudolf Steiner. My appetite to learn more burgeoned. In reflecting on those conversations, I am inclined to say that Rudolf Steiner was our match-maker. Meeting his work was like coming home.

A few years later, when I was pregnant with our first child, my cravings were not the type one usually hears about. No mustard sandwiches or pickles for me. Instead, I wanted to read everything I could find that Steiner had to say about human development. Already grounded by my religious views, I was astonished to learn of a whole other layer—no, multiple layers—of how life works, expands and evolves for every individual and for humanity as a whole. I have now spent almost five decades seeking, pondering, questioning and "wonder"-ing through the extensive works of Rudolf Steiner. His insights not only informed my parenting but set me on a professional path as a teacher/caregiver of young children and educator of others who are parenting, teaching and caring for children.

Let's be clear, however, about one thing. Rudolf Steiner was not, nor did he want to be perceived as, a guru whose word should be taken on faith. His oft-repeated statement was that all he had learned in his spiritual research was available to any and all who are willing to do the work entailed to arrive at such insights. He shared openly and extensively the steps one could take to do so. The starting point, one might say, is to change the way we think. His signature book, the first of what have come to be known as "The Five Basic Books of Anthroposophy," is *The Philosophy of Spiritual Activity*, also known as *The Philosophy of Freedom*. What continues to both perplex and enthrall me is that the spiritual activity he is referring to is "thinking," or best described as *living thinking*, and that freedom is what can manifest in us when we achieve this *living thinking*.

While some seek to understand life through the biological/social science of anthropology, Rudolf Steiner gifted us with a broader and more spiritually oriented science of "anthroposophy," or "the wisdom of the human being." With the ability to perceive the spiritual and physical history of evolution and the future unfolding of humanity, he brought what once seemed too esoteric and mysterious for us commoners right into our living rooms and libraries.

His writings are like living beings, always evolving. In fact, he said as much of his *Philosophy of Freedom*. Talk to anyone who has read this book multiple times, and they will usually tell you that they have found things that they could swear were not there the last time they read it! How well I remember my first reading. We were required to participate in a study group of this text when I was in college in Great Britain, training to become a Waldorf teacher. I literally (really, I mean it!) thought I was going to lose my mind! Perhaps it had as much to do with the participants in my study group as it did with the text, but I would leave class with my head spinning and my world upside down! It was more than two decades before I would pick the book up again, even though I read many other Steiner books with relish. Perhaps age, maturity and life experience helped, but suddenly I found myself actually understanding some of what I was reading! Like others before me and since, I, too, was astonished in subsequent readings to find passages that seemed quite new. I am happy to hear that there is a resurgence of interest in this book and in Rudolf Steiner's works in general.

From such lofty ideals have sprung manifold practical areas of work in the world. As people in the latter years of the 19th century and earliest years of the 20th century became inspired by the knowledge being shared by Steiner, various individuals or groups approached him with specific questions about how to manifest new ways of understanding almost every purposeful activity we do. If *sustainable* is one of the favorite buzzwords of our time, Rudolf Steiner was definitely a century or more ahead of his time! Every ideal or principle for living that he offered had to do with life-sustaining practices in areas as diverse as farming, education, medicine, architecture, religion, arts and music, drama, science, economics and social renewal.

It was quite natural, then, for my colleagues and me in 1998 to turn to Rudolf Steiner's lectures and writings about human development as our guiding star for creating places of care for young children and their families. Now, almost twenty years later, it seems even more important to return to the words and wisdom of Rudolf Steiner to best describe these fundamental needs of children from pre-birth to seven. As mentioned in this book, there is a sweet wholeness to early childhood, and Rudolf Steiner is one of the most profound social scientists to help us understand and appreciate that, for these fresh-from-heaven souls, life is indeed the curriculum.

What do young children need at home and in programs?
A Personal Perspective

What sweet joy it was to observe my two little grandsons, Benjamin, who was three, and Samuel, who was eight months, playing in my living room during a family visit. Ben was playing with anything with which he could weave a story. In one scenario, I was the grocery shop, and a little mouse was the customer. Up and down the grocery aisles (inside my shirtsleeve) went the little mouse, looking for cheese and other good things to eat. Occasionally it would pop its head out to share some important news or to sing a song. After a while the play changed into a puppet show with three wooden sheep—mousey taking a rest—and then it changed to rescue workers in which Ben was the main character, moving around the house "saving the day." Little Sam was playing at learning how to sit up, which he accomplished during the boys' stay at our home. He cut his first tooth as well, and I was certain he had saved these development milestones just for his visit to Gramma's house! What delight!

Ben also helped his Grampa make cinnamon rolls and repair the clothes dryer, played outside, took naps, helped Gramma fix breakfast and sweep the floor, played with a little cousin who came over, and occupied himself with play and more play while the adults were busy doing laundry, paying bills, reading, caring for pets, and performing various other chores. Sam, having accomplished sitting up, started working on his crawling skills, his consonant sounds, and observing his big brother.

Clearly this was a family scene in a family home. It is what we call "everyday life." But is it "everyday life" for the hundreds of thousands of children who spend long hours many days a week with non-family caregivers or in conventional childcare centers? Is it "everyday life" in homes where everyone is out and about most days, where meals are prepared elsewhere, where cleaning and tending to the household happen at times when the children are not around?

Perhaps a more straightforward question is this: Is it "everyday life" for the children in your care? In my care? If we are caring for children, particularly very young children, all day long, are we providing an environment and activities that truly look and feel like home? And does it matter? If it matters, then why? And if *home* is the model, how do we define *home*? If "life" is the curriculum, what are we talking about?

Before we start feeling judged by these questions, let's explore them. Let's consider what/if/how the conventions of "home-life" and "home-making" make sense (or not) for the modern family, and more specifically, the young child.

Recognizing a Change

It was surprising to me how many changes were necessary when, in 1998, I started caring for children all day as compared to providing morning kindergarten only. My kindergarten within a Waldorf school had gone from 8:30 to noon every day from September to early June and was mostly comprised of the children playing inside and outside, experiencing circle games and stories, crafting or doing some artistic work, helping to make bread or mid-morning snack, cleaning the room together every Friday, and celebrating festivals throughout the year. I loved it, and if I were still in a morning-only kindergarten, I would mostly continue to do things that way.

Early in my career, I felt happy knowing that after kindergarten most of the children were going home for lunch and a rest, followed by a free-flowing afternoon of play while the adults tended to household matters and personal interests. Then everything changed. For a variety of reasons, most children were no longer spending much of their day at home. Articles, even books, have been written about this cultural paradigm shift. It became imperative to pause, to take several deep breaths, and to contemplate what this shift means for our children. And what does this shift mean for the adults caring for the children?

These questions are still being explored. We are, and we need to be, in an ongoing state of open listening and astute observing of the children, the parents and ourselves as caregivers and teachers. To do what we have always done may or may not be working. I can honestly say that when I started caring for infants and two-year-olds along with three-, four- and five-year-olds, what I had been doing in my kindergarten was no longer what was most needed.

The older children still needed artistic experiences, stories and games, festival celebrations, and all the components mentioned above. But the context had changed. More than anything, they also needed simplicity, room to breathe, slowing down, and less of almost everything! The beauty of mixing them with the youngest children was that the needs of the younger children automatically required that things simplify and slow down. It also required that the group sizes be smaller and more family-like.

And how is it for the adults who are providing the care? I cannot answer that question for anyone other than myself (and individuals who have shared their experiences with me). It is like a most amazing, ongoing research project. The answers vary somewhat according to the ideology out of which a person works. One finds a level of resonance toward simplicity when conversing with professionals and parents inspired by Rudolf Steiner, Maria Montessori, Friedrich Fröbel, Jean Piaget, the Reggio Emilia work in Italy, and others who recognized the time and uncluttered life children need when first learning about the world. We find it again within the content offered by modern child development experts such as David Elkind, Joseph Chilton Pearce, Bruce Perry and Berry Brazelton, just to name a few. In their works we also find something else that resonates with the ideals presented by Rudolf Steiner, namely, the crucial component of relationship-based care, which will be explored further below.

When Steiner (or Waldorf) kindergartens were first developed, there were few, if any, concrete suggestions from Rudolf Steiner as to what we should be doing with the child prior to elementary school. Rather, we received a profound overview of development in early childhood, out of which we could decide how best to serve young children. Over time various forms and activities became common practice, although always individually articulated by the particular teacher within the confines of a particular geographic location.

Now we are at a new threshold. While there are some Steiner childcare providers who have been working with very young children in all-day care for many years, within the context of the Steiner education movement, this is still relatively new work. We have learned that, in working with children under three and also in our parent-child work, pressing down the forms and schedules once found in the kindergarten does not serve the children's needs. Parents are not in need of learning how to create a kindergarten experience for their children. They need to know how to set up a meaningful home life. Infants, toddlers and two-year-olds need a different pace and daily content than in the typical kindergarten. And children who are in all-day care—even the three- to six-year-olds—need experiences found in daily home life because the care setting is their "home" for a good part of their week.

Let's take this opportunity to look anew at the essentials. Can we look afresh, as if we were just now being asked to establish daily care for young children in our own homes or in care settings and early childhood programs? Can we pretend that there have been no others before us to articulate programs or schedules, that all we have are the developmental pictures so profoundly articulated by Rudolf Steiner in his lectures, articles and books?

Let us go on a journey together, as if we are hearing Steiner's ideals for the first time. And from these developmental insights, let us consider fundamentals of care for children and families. Our purpose will not be to discover a blueprint or a singular way to create programs or care settings.

Decades ago, as a student at Emerson College in England and doing my practicum at Michael Hall Steiner School in the kindergartens, I remember being astonished at how different each of the four kindergartens looked and felt. I remember feeling that each had its own rightfulness according to the teacher's sensibilities and dedication to the children in her care.

Similarly, in establishing home-away-from-home care for infants, toddlers and the full mix of ages in early childhood, we can expect and hope to find variations from one place to the next. Just as family homes differ according to the inner lives and outer practices of the parents, so shall it be in our care settings. What we strive for, as common purpose, is to meet the developmental needs of the children out of the profound indications offered to us through spiritual science as indicated by Rudolf Steiner. In doing this we will explore four categories:

Life as Curriculum
Child as Curriculum
Adult as Curriculum/Child as Apprentice
Environment as Curriculum

Quotes from Rudolf Steiner will be followed by a few insights gained by observing in early childhood homes and centers in the last two decades. The book or lecture series from which each quote is taken is given after the quote. After each section you will be invited to contemplate, through a few questions, how these ideals might affect your own care of children, whether as a caregiver or as a parent in your own home.

1

Life as Curriculum

The task of the kindergarten [early childhood] teacher is to
adopt the practical activities of daily life so that they are suitable
for the child's imitation through play.... The activities of children in
kindergarten [early childhood] must be derived directly
from life itself rather than being "thought out" by
the intellectualized culture of adults.

RUDOLF STEINER, FROM *THE CHILD'S CHANGING CONSCIOUSNESS*

When, in our first LifeWays childcare center, we explored what it meant to
care for children all day long and all week long, we felt it was essential that
the flow of the day be as reflective as possible of a day in the life of a
household. We wanted the shift from parents to caregivers to feel similar
to arriving at a favorite aunt's or grandparent's house with warmth and welcome. While it was essential to have a clearly laid out schedule and
daily/weekly rhythms, we also wanted a feeling of the spontaneity of home
that was not overbooked with set activities. We also asked ourselves, what
were *the activities derived from life itself*, as noted by Steiner? As we as-
sessed what would happen in the children's day, we arrived at practices we
called the *Living Arts*. These life arts can be grouped into four categories:

23

Practical, Domestic Activity. This category includes so many things—washing dishes, food preparation, cleaning and caring for the environment, laundry, gardening, paying bills, repairing things, car maintenance, yard care, animal care, and a myriad of daily deeds that keep things afloat! In fact, over the years, workshop participants and our students have created a list of twenty-two practical activities that help to maintain a household, and we all agree it is surely not a complete list!

We do not expect the children to participate in all of these activities, although they often want to; rather, we provide for them a model of life where the adults are fully engaged in those activities that "make life work." Whether or not the children participate directly, they participate inwardly, experiencing the purposefulness, presence and interest of the adults, and they often imitate the activities in their play. When people first hear the concept, they think it will be quite labor intensive for the caregiver or parent or even for the child. However, what we have found is that being really present in doing things of a transformative nature can feel like an elixir to adults. And the "curriculum of life" is always full of possibility; one does not need to do a lot of clever constructing of less meaningful "stuff."

Another benefit is that children learn about processes. Imagine realizing that dirty laundry does not just get put into a basket and then magically show up clean later. These children see all the steps take place before their eyes—sorting, washing, drying, sometimes ironing, folding and putting away! Being able to follow process is a highly valued executive function! This is an important thing to share with parents or policy makers who are concerned that domestic activity should not be a part of a child's daily curriculum in preschool. Indeed, it is one of the most brilliant constructs for learning and, as a side benefit, the environment has been well tended!

Nurturing Care. As a kindergarten teacher, I remember the year I had over twenty children in my class who arrived each day with gusto like a flock of wild, running ducks! That was the year I introduced hair brushing at the start of the morning. A calm tenderness came over the room as each little head was gently stroked and we all settled in for a story that helped us transition from whatever chaotic encounters the morning had offered to a mood of quiet listening. Of course a time for robust play came later in the morning, but recognizing the need for personal touch as children left the family to find themselves suddenly with a large group of children was as essential as making sure they had good food to eat. When I started working with smaller, mixed-age groups of children, the need for tender, loving care did not diminish, particularly as many of them were with us for longer days.

We know that bonding is crucial for the health and well-being of the young child, and one of the best ways to bond with another person is through loving touch. Of course, there is also the need for hygienic care throughout the day with children—washing hands and faces, toileting, diapering, and tending to booboos. Therapeutic touch also can be incorporated—including warm foot baths, gentle caresses, rocking, cuddling, massaging, touching games that help to settle a child toward sleep or robust bouncing games that delight the toddler. In fact, workshop participants and students came up with twenty nurturing care activities that seemed important to bestow in the course of the day or week with young children. This included a few things that cross over into the next category—creative exploration—for music, stories, puppet plays and games can also be considered nurturing.

Creative Exploration and Skill Development. "If music be the food of love, play on," wrote Shakespeare. In caring for young children, it becomes apparent that artistic endeavor is not only a way to express love, but also a way to offer solid ground from which an individual's creative genius may spring. In early childhood, it is simply a different type of creative play, with skill-building being a byproduct of giving children the opportunity to explore artistic materials regularly.

By offering creative crafting in relationship to the festival celebrations throughout the year, we discovered that we were not imitating the "make-and-take" modality so popular in conventional childcare, in which adults expect children to take home some project almost every day, even if it is nothing more than cotton balls glued onto construction paper. Rather, we found that by using beautiful materials and giving children time to create something lovely over a period of days or weeks, a true sense of beauty and purpose existed in whatever the children crafted. Watercolor paintings became beautiful gift cards or paper lanterns, for example. As the children grew older, simple woodworking projects or learning how to finger crochet served as markers to the children that they were moving toward a new phase in which fine motor skills would open up worlds of possibility.

Of equal or even greater importance, we encourage caregivers and parents to become skilled in arts and crafts so the children see beautiful and practical items being created for the home or childcare center. When not tending to the practical, domestic needs of the day, spending time doing a favorite activity or artistic endeavor is a splendid way to relax and model for children that such activities are meaningful.

Social Awareness. "Play is the highest expression of human development in childhood, for it alone is the free expression of what is in a child's soul." This quote from kindergarten pioneer Friedrich Fröbel resonates deeply with the core of how we approach the *Living Arts* with children, for if we leave them to their own way of expressing life, we will see a playful impulse in practically all of their deeds. It is through play that they develop social awareness and move through the stages of playing alone to side-by-side play, to friend play, and then to group play. Throughout this progression, conflict and its resolution result in growing levels of social awareness.

Blessed are the children who have the opportunity to observe adults engaging in all of these stages of play as well! When a caregiver or parent meets a project or artistic craft with joyful anticipation (maybe getting a few rows crocheted on the next set of wash cloths or baking a cake for a friend), the children are taking in her attitude. When two or more adults (parents, grandparents, caregivers or teachers) are working side by side to care for children and they share a moment of levity with one another, it is

fun to observe the children. They will often imitate the laughter or facial expressions of the adults.

When, in the midst of a focused activity, an unexpected visitor shows up (be it a friend, neighbor, repair person or delivery person), the children closely observe and drink in how their caregivers meet the interruption. Are they able to overcome their frustration and meet the person with calm dignity, or are they rude out of a level of exhaustion they have been able to mask until that unexpected moment? Whatever happens, the children will likely imitate it in their play with each other or even with their dolls. However, it is also a gift to the children to see an adult do what the old song says: "Pick yourself up, dust yourself off, and start all over again." There will be plenty of other opportunities to model one's highest and best in a future encounter. Perfection is not our goal. Seeing us in our own striving is

a form of social awareness we hope the children will emulate as they grow. Being with a group of adults, whether during mundane tasks or at celebratory gatherings, can be favorite times for young children who want to meet the world. Even the shy, quiet child can be seen tucking herself or himself into a lap or quiet corner and savoring the parade of humanity. The more robust child thrills at those times when the adults join in a game or folk dancing or a festive celebration. It is as if the children are inoculated by our attitude toward life.

All of these *Living Arts* are meant to serve the health and well-being of the twelve senses and especially the four bodily senses (touch, life, movement and balance) discussed by Rudolf Steiner. A lovely side-effect has been the number of caregivers who have told us how much more they enjoy their lives and their work since they expanded their days and/or changed to a life-based approach. *Home Away from Home* offers a window into a day in the life of a childcare home or center based on these *Living Arts* in chapter one and provides further discussion of the living arts in chapter four.

> You know children do what they see grownups do, but they do it in a different way. Their play is far removed from the purpose and usefulness with which adults connect sense activities. It is only the formal side of adult activity which is imitated by the child, not the material side. Its usefulness is absent; the child pursues no definite purpose. Akin to what in the adult is purpose in the child is the sense of satisfaction.
>
> —Rudolf Steiner, quoted in *Understanding Young Children*, from the *Basel Course on Pedagogy*

When my young grandson helped to crack the eggs for breakfast, he did not inquire about next steps or what else was needed or even when we were going to eat. When he helped with the repair of the clothes dryer, he did not wait around to see that it worked. However, one could sense his satisfaction by observing the deep play that followed those activities. In family-style childcare, we have also observed this. We encourage the caregivers to be actively involved with meal preparation even if there is a professional cook who puts the final meal together for everyone. Caregivers also do as much of the laundry as possible and tend to the cleaning and caring of their environments, even though a professional cleaning service may come in over the weekend. It is delightful when the children participate in these activities. In reality, however, we are providing them opportunities to enter into deep, satisfying play. Being present and focused in our own activity helps the children to be more present and focused in their play. Sometimes their play is an imitation of the work they have experienced us doing—cooking, cleaning, tending to a baby or repairing things, for example. They set up their play houses, shops and doll nurseries accordingly.

If, on the other hand, the caregivers do not find their own delight in house-tending or homemaking but do it only to "model" for the children, it is less likely to have the same satisfying effect on the children. Finding delight in meaningful practical work sounds like an oxymoron in today's prevailing culture. But try it! Sing, hum or even whistle while you work if that helps. Become interested in the fact that you are involved with real transformation. Notice the uplifting feeling that you, and others, have when you walk into a freshly cleaned or tidied space. What is that? Some-thing has been lifted—that is transformation. And when we adults can find a positive relationship to our work, it becomes more authentic to who we are and, thus, more attractive to the children in our care.

As the children grow older, particularly when we are fortunate enough to retain a few five- or six-year-olds, they may be more interested in all the steps of an activity and perhaps even inquire as to the end results. Here one can catch a glimpse of the child moving from the age of imitation to the eagerness to trust the authority of the adult.

He wants to do what he sees being done in his immediate sur-roundings. But what he does must be connected with life; it must be led over into living activity. We can do very much to help bring this about if we accustom the child to feel gratitude for what he receives from this world; if, in confronting the outer world and wanting to imitate it, the child sees the kind of gestures that express gratitude, then a great deal is done toward establishing in him the right moral human attitude.

—Rudolf Steiner, in *Human Values in Education*

Children, whose senses are so completely open, can discern when an adult is doing something out of drudgery or doing it out of interest and with gratitude. This discernment is not experienced in an intellectualized manner.

The young child feels, in his body, the inner mood and intention of the adult. How we tend to our tools—brooms, mops, laundry basket, diaper pail, toilet brush, kitchen appliances and such—is one way we can exhibit gratitude. Do we place things back where we found them, or do we toss them into the closet without much care? Do we scrub the table helter-skelter, or do we have an easy flow to our movement? Our physical gestures when we are cleaning and caring speak volumes to the child. Even the infants may become agitated if they sense that we are frustrated by the incessant tending required to maintain a "household." Of course, most of us are not yet perfect! When we fall from grace or from the standards we have set for ourselves, the children are well served when they experience us taking a deep breath, pausing to reassess the situation, and perhaps even having a little chuckle over our human frailties. It is amazing how healing a little humor can be. What a delightful guffaw and belly laugh my great-nephew and I had recently when I completely and unwittingly messed up the music lesson we were having together!

It is not only our attitude of gratitude in relationship to our work that the children notice. More overt expressions of gratitude are observed in the way we meet and greet the other adults in the environment, whether it be the appliance repair person, a fellow caregiver/teacher, the cook or the parents. Why do we hear adults so often telling children to say *thank you* when they rarely think to say it themselves to the people to whom they are the closest—partners and colleagues?

> And the moment a child perceives something, whether it be a movement, or whether it be a sound, there arises in him the impulse of an inward gesture, to re-live what has been perceived with the whole intensity of his inner nature.
>
> —Rudolf Steiner, in *Understanding Young Children*, from *Spiritual Ground of Education*, Oxford

When life is the curriculum, the experiences life requires vary according to the ages of the people involved. Practical, domestic activities may remain the same, for the most part; however, when an infant is around, schedules shift and the whole household softens regarding movement and noise levels. When the baby is sleeping at the time we normally vacuum the floor, we make adjustments. When we are diapering a child and another child is observing, we recognize that both children are drinking in the warmth-imbued gestures. We also find that having family-sized groupings of children, rather than institutional-sized groupings, is much less overwhelming for all of the ages. The infants and the toddlers are not as overstimulated; in fact, being with a few older children who tend to have a protective gesture toward them can be less stressful than being with only same-age children. The sounds of the singing games and stories of the older children can be soothing or delightful to the younger ones. The older children thrive in an environment where they are less likely to feel the need to "run with the pack," having the opportunity to enter into deeper play with fewer children. Knowing that every sound and movement is a stimulant to the young child encourages simplicity in the schedule and daily routines.

Don't we experience this also as adults? Sometime, when you create a moment to be still at the end of a day, explore what it is in you that is tired. Can you learn to discern the difference between body-weary and mind-weary or spirit-weary? See if you can figure out why making time to do creative cooking and slow-paced chores can be emotionally invigorating as compared to a day of edutainment, listening to rapid-fire conversation, and moving constantly from one activity to another.

Children thrive in a sense of timelessness, and that requires not overloading the day with too much flotsam and jetsam. Truth time: We adults thrive in less also. And some compatriots have found that the world continues to revolve even when we slow down and simplify!

> **The child needs so much sleep because he is entirely sense-organ, because he could not otherwise endure the dazzle and noise of the outer world.**
>
> —Rudolf Steiner, in *Understanding Young Children*,
> from *Spiritual Ground of Education*, Oxford

Modern life, as we know, is full of dazzle and noise. Silence is rare, even in a typical home because of the quiet electrical buzz of the fridge or hot water heater or washing machine. We recently experienced a several-hour power outage. Something edging toward silence and stillness began to pervade our house. It felt like our home got to have a big exhale.

When, added to the regular background noise of a conventional household, there are often two or more computers, a large-screen television, and the beeps and blips of modern kitchen appliances, quiet becomes even more elusive. Perhaps this is why many parents today feel a need to have a white noise machine in their child's room. It may be an attempt to overshadow all of the other household sounds. It may also be a result of a growing discomfort with quiet. Many adults fall asleep to background noise and assume it will be easier for their infant or child also to sleep with soft noise. Our childcare settings are not monasteries. They certainly have their share of ambient noise. With family-sized groups of children, there is plenty of sound coming from their daily play and social exchanges. However, they are the noises of life rather than another machine-noise trying to mask it. Certainly at sleep time, a deeper level of quiet is pursued, and sleepiness tends to pervade the space.

With a family mix, an infant may be sleeping while the children are playing in the next room or outside. At group nap time, it is not unusual for an infant to be sleeping at that same time. The baby's morning nap begins to adjust in such a way that he or she is ready for a second nap at the regular nap time. This is a gradual process. Much attention and intention is given to the sleep of the children. Jaimmie Stugard, a longtime caregiver, has created a DVD (available at www.lifewaysnorthamerica.org) on the subject of sleep and how to frame the nap experience in a successful way. It involves increasing awareness of transitions from playtime to mealtime, toileting and tooth brushing with awareness, preparing the nap space, preparing one's inner life for peace and quiet, and thinking the transitions all the way through to what happens as soon as the first child awakens.

We have also discovered great benefit in spending a few moments during naptime to reconnect to each child's angel. As you gaze at a child, beholding her or his wholeness, take a moment to partner in a profound way with the spiritual being most connected to that child. And what a great partnership to cultivate for those befuddled days when you cannot figure out what in the world needs to be done for a child gone rogue! What guardian angel wouldn't want to send an inspirational thought to a person unabashedly devoted to that child?!

It has surprised some caregivers to discover that having a somewhat longer day with the children, rather than just the morning, leaves them feeling more relaxed and that the days have a more natural, organic flow. It feels more like living with the children and less like creating a program for them, and this restful nap break after lunch can become a mainstay in helping caregivers and teachers feel that their work is sustainable.

Regarding the *dazzle* of life, the choices made for the visual appearance of the care setting are of equal import to tending the noise level. More will be said about this in another section, but it is important to note that one of the reasons we highly value spending time outside with the children is to give their sense organs (and ours) ample opportunity to breathe and relax in unadulterated nature.

Ponderables

◎ What is your relationship to daily life tasks—cooking, cleaning, tidying, repairing and such? If you want to make changes, list three things you will start doing (or stop doing, if that be the case).

◎ Do you remember feeling rushed as a child? Or did you feel your days were fairly even-paced? List three things you could change in your daily schedule in order to stop feeling rushed.

◎ How do you feel about children participating in your daily work? Are you fine with them playing while you work, or do you want them to be involved all the time? Would you prefer that they were not involved?

◎ Do you see value in exposing children to the practical activities that make a household function?

◎ Do you have a rest time midday? Even when the children are not there? Can you rest (read, daydream, breathe deeply)—even for a while— while the children rest?

◎ Have you found that if you slow down and rest a bit, this helps the children to rest? In the next two weeks, rest for a time while the children are resting and see what a difference it makes in your energy and efficiency.

⊚ What is your nap routine? Is it working? List one thing you could change to make it work more effectively.

2

Child as Curriculum

They arrive with their own laws of individuality, their own being,
and their own history, which reaches far into the past—
much farther than the day of their birth
and the nine months of pregnancy.

—PETER SELG, IN *UNBORNNESS*
(BASED ON THE RESEARCH OF RUDOLF STEINER)

When parents have more than one child, they are often surprised that each can be such a unique individual. How well I remember being shocked that so little of what I did with my first son in the realm of guidance worked at all with my second son. However, in reflecting on the differences in the pregnancies, in the births, in the way they each slept, in how they took their first steps, and so on, it began to make sense. To this day, as adults, they continue to be as different as Jupiter and Mars. My own mother was noting the other day how extremely different her three daughters are from one another. She said, "You all ate the same food and grew up in the same household!"

Do such extreme differences among children raised similarly strike you

as odd? Could it be that something other than heredity and family culture has made an equally strong imprint on each child? What is this "history which reaches far into the past" to which Peter Selg is referring? How can a very young child already have a history?

Have you ever been caught in the gaze of an infant and had the feeling that someone with depth and breadth, character and clarity, knowings and wonderings was staring at you? It may have been for only a brief moment, but you felt a quickening in your soul, didn't you? "Who are you?" you may have wanted to say. But the answer to that question is not really what matters. What matters is whether or not you are willing to entertain the thought that this fresh, innocent one in your arms is already Some One. And it is no accident that she or he is in your arms in that moment and has come to learn from and teach you in the Vast Unfolding.

The young child is both individual and universal from the very beginning. There are archetypal developmental milestones we come to expect in every typically developing child. In that, we might say, "all babies are alike"; they are universal. But we know we would be wrong to say only that, especially in our current times when the gaze of many infants comes earlier and earlier. And if we are paying close attention, we may also notice subtle differences in how they move, what makes them feel soothed, when they cut their first teeth, what sorts of sounds attract their attention, and any number of other things. As caregivers and teachers, this is one of the crucial reasons it can be so helpful to hear about the births of the children in our care when possible. An individual's birth story often has a theme repeated throughout his or her life.

My firstborn was one of those star-gazing newborns, face-up in the birth canal and none too eager to emerge. Sigh.... (Mothers who have delivered a baby like this know why I am sighing!) Throughout his young childhood, he took his time entering into social situations and new experiences. Over time, however, his interests in music, drama and philosophy have played an important role in his work as a public speaker and facilitator for community colleges and work force development. Our second child shot into the world in less than an hour of labor and, even as a toddler, gave the impression of being in control of the situation, organizing much older children on the playground. An accomplished athlete in his youth, he continues to enjoy adventure (as does his brother, actually) and runs his own finance business. Each of these young men is accomplished in life—in work, in parenting, in community, and in passion for what he deems important.

An interesting side note is that the son who was slow to enter the world was "on target" or "early" with many of the physical developmental milestones, whereas the rocket child took his time with some things. How do we account for this if we do not trust in *laws of individuality*?

If we become too attached to the image of the archetype, we can find ourselves becoming diagnosticians, labeling as a "problem" something which may be merely a mark of that being's individuality. If we are bold enough to embrace the spiritual scientific view of world evolution and individual karma and destiny, it becomes more clear that a child bearing the past experience of a Napoleonic nature might move, speak and behave quite differently from someone like Hildegard of Bingen. A person whose future destiny involves physical prowess and strength might be seeking different childhood experiences from someone who is moving toward a path of quiet contemplation and literature. This does not give us license to ignore or enable destructive behavior or inhibited social ability, but it gives us pause to reflect on the fact that we are participants in the unfolding lives of eternally evolving beings. What is good for one is not always good for all (and vice versa)!

On the other hand, we also want to become deeply familiar with archetypal child development in order to bring depth and clarity to how we conduct our lives in the presence of these young souls. For instance, if we do not understand that infants have primitive reflexes and need protection from extremely loud noises or being manipulated into physical positions which they are not ready to achieve for themselves, this oversight can be as disturbing to the child as our lack of awareness of his or her individuality.

> The soul and spirit forces which work in the building up of the body until the seventh year are called by Dr. Steiner "formative forces." It is apparent to spiritual scientific investigation that they are already present before birth. In conception they are brought down into earthly existence; they shape the physical, bodily organism and emerge on their release as faculties of thought and memory.
>
> —Editor, in *Understanding Young Children*

Dr. Steiner offered a clear understanding of how the formative forces (the etheric stream of forces that support the physical body) are particularly important during the first seven years. Primarily, in the first two years or so, the focus is on developing the nerve-sense system; from a bit over two to around five, the rhythmic system; and from around five to seven, the limb/metabolic system. Knowing how these forces work in the early years can increase our resolve that whatever we do with the infants and toddlers needs to have a repetitive quality, even paying attention that we change an infant's diaper as much as possible in the same way each time or that we help the toddler get dressed in the same progression each time. Such routines are healthy and predictable, soothing to the nervous system and supportive of healthy brain development. This remains true throughout all of early childhood.

In the middle phase of early childhood we take extra care that not only the physical bodily care we offer, but also the musicality of the child's experience through stories, games and songs provides a rhythmical experience that encompasses "in and out," "up and down," "fast and slow," "quiet and loud" and other polarities of rhythm. What we discover is a beneficial way to focus on the unfolding day, the unfolding week and the unfolding season, each with slightly different intentions. The daily focus is built around eating and sleeping. The weekly focus is built around the chosen *Living Arts* activities that want to happen as the week unfolds. Looking in this way, we recognized that some things we had been doing every day with the children, such as multiple adult-led activities, were actually creating a sense of overwhelm in both the children and the adults. By spreading these activities over the week, taking into consideration the nature of each day (Monday/Moon Day is not the same as Wednesday/Mercury Day), certain activities are carefully chosen to fill in the times between eating and sleeping on particular days. We also discovered that some artistic activities, such as watercolor painting or crafts, were well served within the context of seasonal/festival life rather than feeling that we needed to paint or do a craft project every week.

In that third phase of early childhood, five-and-a-half to seven, we build upon the routines created to strengthen the nerve/sense system; remain dedicated to sensible, not too overwhelming rhythms for the rhythmic system; and bring joyful intention to a variety of movement experiences and awareness of healthy digestion, not only of food but of life activities. When we are fortunate enough to retain a few five- or six-year-olds (since many parents send them on to school by that time), it is such fun to see how they achieve tree climbing, jumping rope, more delicate handwork capacities, skilled food preparations with knives and such, and other bodily achievements.

The beauty of having mixed ages is the natural picture and experience of unfolding life. While it is unusual in the Western world to experience many families with six to eight children (and even fewer with ten or twelve!), one can imagine how it is for the older ones to observe the awakening skills of the little ones while the little ones experience the refinement of the skills of their older "siblings."

> [I]n the child everything is carried out in a more living and animated way than with the adult, because the child is still a unity in body, soul and spirit. In the adult the body has been freed from the soul and spirit, and the soul and spirit from the body. Body, soul and spirit stand side by side as single entities; in the child they are firmly united. This unity even penetrates into the thinking....
>
> —Rudolf Steiner, from *The Kingdom of Childhood*

In a post on a Waldorf Early Childhood chat group, long-time early childhood teacher Sarah Hummingbird noted: "By the way, I had a barometer in my house, and I came to believe that when there's a drop in barometric pressure, the children are less resilient within themselves. I've also noticed this with cats, who would run circles around the house before a storm!"

It is essential that we pause when we are observing children's behavior. When we note something happening *en masse*, it is a good idea to look at what is happening in the larger cultural context, whether it be weather, social uprisings, political upheaval or any number of other things that can influence the child's sense of well-being. If it is the behavior of a single child, we need to consider what is happening in the child's individual culture. Young children "think" with their bodies. Even now, when children have become more expressively verbal than in decades past, it still holds true that their body reactions can tell us volumes about how they are processing their lives.

Particularly when our care becomes "home away from home" for a child, it is important for all the adults to know all of the children. Just as in a family, when an auntie or uncle may see something that a primary parent has not digested, the same can be true with a group of caregivers. In the Milwaukee LifeWays Early Childhood Center in Wisconsin, the caregivers visit with each other almost every day after their children have fallen asleep. I have observed how they bring concerns to one another and how, as a group, they carry all the children in their care. And like a neighborhood, a child from one group may "visit" another group for a bit of playtime. Perhaps you remember from your own childhood how something could be diffused if you just went next door for a while or spent an afternoon with your grandma. Children need a "break" now and then, just like we do!

When we take the time to observe how a child processes life, we also understand more about how and why she or he enters into certain activities with specific movements or gestures. While attending a wonderful marionette workshop several years ago, I looked across the table at a beloved colleague crafting her puppet and saw how she held her body a particular way and how her tongue was often peeking out of the side of her mouth when she was maneuvering her needle at certain angles. It was, for me, like looking in a mirror, as I have retained that same gesture from my childhood. It is almost as if my tongue becomes another limb, bringing just the right balance to my actions. Recognizing this in myself helps me to recognize such actions in young children who "think" with their bodies.

An important advantage of truly getting to know all the children in your care is that you come to know when a child's behavior is a reflection of how she or he processes activities as compared to when behavior is active defiance. The child who tosses the wash cloths up in the air and then puts them over her face before finally folding them may be doing early childhood *science* with the laundry! Think of all the concepts her body just experienced (not with the adult intellect but with her body intellect). Remember *"in the child everything is carried out in a more living and animated way than with the adult."*

∞

> [Regarding learning to walk and speak:] Here again the rule holds good that we should leave everything to the child itself. Of its own accord it will raise itself to an upright position when the right time comes.
>
> —Rudolf Steiner, in *Understanding Young Children*

What a wonderfully simple and straightforward statement Rudolf Steiner offers us here. We feel affirmed in our awareness that our little ones do not need the popular "equipment" of the times in order to develop physically. It is highly unlikely that a baby walker would ever be found in a Steiner-based early care center. When we consider the topic of environments, below, we can look at this further.

There has been an interesting dialogue among infant caregivers about how one places a baby on the floor or in the crib. Magda Gerber (magda gerber.org), who was inspired by Emmi Pikler (pikler.org), suggested that a child should always be placed on the back, where it looks more naturally comfortable. Some pediatricians, however, have noted an increase in flat-headedness where the backs of infants' heads are flattened, partly due to the amount of time they are pressed against infant seats and also because of the increase in sleeping only on the back. Others, such as Sally Goddard Blythe (sallygoddardblythe.co.uk), recommend tummy time wherein the child's efforts to lift the head and upper body against gravity help to develop the compound sense of body map. Some specialists question whether certain developmental learning delays, including speech delays, present in primary school age children have to do with weakened upper body capacity. From a lecture by Dr. Steiner in Dornach, April 1923, we learn that "the relation between physical equilibrium (action of the legs) and psychical equilibrium (action of the hands and arms) forms the foundation which enables the child to come into contact with the outer world through the

Through educated observation, devotion and love,

tain for the young child how, when, and how muc'

time serve his or her long-term physical and emot'

In the meantime, we can take care not to rush upright... the infant before she can walk on her own. We also avoid rolling a baby ov... when fussy about being "stuck" in the halfway position—that is, unless the infant is extremely upset or frightened. And we must pay attention that the environment provides space for the newly mobile crawler or creeper. We have learned in our childcare settings that whenever there is a child who is learning to pull up in our midst, then the pretty cloths on the nature table or the long tablecloth on the dining table are best left off for a while. Not unlike in the family home, the setting is adjusted to the safety and well-being of the youngest. This also provides respite to the caregiver who, knowing that the environment is safe, no longer needs to hover near the child.

> In the less well-behaved children who make a great deal of
> healthy noise, who shout properly and give a lot of trouble,
> the spirit is active, though of course in a clumsy way, for it has
> been transported from heaven to earth, but the spirit is active
> within them. It is making use of the body. We may even regard
> the wild screams of a child as most enthralling.... Of course,
> we must follow the conventions to some extent and not allow
> all naughtiness to pass unreproved.
>
> —Rudolf Steiner, in *The Kingdom of Childhood*

We have developed an approach to discipline or child guidance based on eight aspects of human awareness. Called the L.O.V.E. approach to discipline, it includes *listening, laughter, objectivity, order, versatility, vulnerability, energy and enthusiasm*. There are many tools available in each of these categories; however, the number one tool is training oneself always to remember the spiritual nature of the young child. The overly reserved, quiet child sometimes requires a more complicated, long-term effort of support. Rather than trying to "push" this child into social play, we might instead engage her physically in the practical activities of home life or in the nurturing care of another child. Bringing her every day into physical movement often leads to the inner soul movement that allows her to enter later into deep play. In my next-to-last year as a kindergarten teacher, one of the children, Katherine, was seemingly glued to me every day. No matter how I tried to encourage her into playing with the other children, in moments she was back at my side. I finally accepted this as her life gesture at that time and simply involved her in whatever I was doing. The following year, one of my greatest parting gifts was observing this same child as the leader of the pack! She knew the activities and routines of the kindergarten from the inside out, and I almost sensed I could have turned the class over to her! She had not been "doing nothing" the previous year; rather, she had been drinking it all in in her own quiet way.

I learned so much from Katherine about the importance of extending as much care and concern to the quiet child as to the wild, attention-grabbing child. The active child, so beautifully illustrated in the above quote by Dr. Steiner, strengthens the creativity of the adults. He requires us to examine the flow of the day, the appropriate set up of the rooms and furniture, the quality and nature of the meals, and the exploration of ourselves in relation to personal flexibility, inner life and outer gesture.

With the construct of the "loving wall" [represented by the inner knowing of the adult], one can send compassion and care toward an aggressive child while at the same time bringing calm clarity to the fact that the "loving wall" is indeed a wall, a boundary that is there for good reason. My first gray hair arrived the same year that Elijah came into the kindergarten. Never still and very destructive to the physical space, he taught me the importance of meditating upon a child and asking for help from all who would listen! The leading partners in his care included his dedicated parents, my wonderful kindergarten assistant, and Elijah's guardian angel. By learning how to assess his trigger points, making sure he had enough very active outside play, and holding up a consistent "loving wall," we all survived that year. The following year his destructive nature had calmed considerably, and he was able to participate in circle games and other activities that previously had sent him into chaos. The beauty of being in a profession for a long time is that one can share the fruits born of experience. Encountering both Katherine and Elijah as adults, I am pleased to report that their lives are filled with meaning and purpose and the ability to navigate whatever comes their way.

Ponderables

◎ Learn about the birth story of two children you know and see if you can sense the gesture of their births in their behavior in life. Do the same thing with two children in middle childhood and then with two adults. It is not a hard and fast rule, but it is interesting to explore.

◎ Read or review several texts on the archetypal development of the child from birth to age three. Suggested texts include: Rudolf Steiner's *Education of the Child*, Karl König's *The First Three Years* (chapters on Movement, Speech and Thinking), and *Understanding Young Children, A Compilation* by Rudolf Steiner. For slightly less esoteric content, there are many wonderful articles in the *Waldorf Early Childhood Digest* "Developing Child, The First Seven Years." Some people also enjoy the series of photographs Barbara Patterson used in *Beyond the Rainbow Bridge* or Joan Salter's series in *The Incarnating Child*. Some caregivers have found the more conventional textbook *Developmental Profiles from Pre-Birth to Twelve* by K. Eileen Allen and Lynn R. Marotz to be helpful. After reading some of these, observe three children in the birth-to-three age range and watch them objectively. Do you see resonance with what you have read regarding archetypal movement and behavior? What did you see that appeared more individualized, less archetypal, in the children you observed?

◎ Observe an infant gazing for a period of time. Observe a toddler studying a toy or an object in nature. Can you perceive what is happening in their nerve/sense organization? Observe a child in the three-to-five age range watching a puppet show, playing a circle game, or listening to a story. Can you perceive how well the child's rhythmic system is served through the repetition and appropriate pacing of these activities, particularly if he gets to experience them several times over a period of days or weeks? Observe a child in the five-to-seven age range playing outside or involved in a building project or a fine motor activity such as finger crochet or sewing. Compared to the younger child, can you perceive the emerging bodily skills in the child's hands and limbs, even if still a bit clumsy?

◎ Observe a group of children involved with cleaning up a space. What different characteristics of movement do you see that illustrate the quality of wholeness to which Rudolf Steiner refers when he states that the young child is a unity in body, soul and spirit?

◎ Observe yourself for a week while caring for your children. How often do you find yourself interfering with their self-directed movement or play (for example, rescuing an infant who is trying to pull up by standing her up yourself, or making suggestions for play themes instead of leaving the child or children to come up with their own ideas, regardless of how clumsy they are socially)? Write down two or three things you can do to help yourself stop interfering and review them before going to sleep and upon waking each day.

◎ What does your "loving wall" look like regarding discipline? Think of three ways you could meet a discipline situation with a child in a more healthy way than your current practice. Would humor help? A little story? Involving the child in an activity? Changing the scene? Standing matter-of-factly in the clarity of "we are doing this now"? What else might you try? Picture these more creative approaches in your mind with as much detail as possible. Describe them to a trusted friend, partner or colleague. Practice the new approach by acting it out privately (even in front of a mirror) or with a partner. Do this a few times before you actually try it out with the child. Don't worry if it doesn't work the first time, but don't be surprised if it does!

A Word about Infants in Care

Our strength trainer introduced an exercise he called *easy rolls* to my husband and me in our first weeks of working with him. Of course, he knew it was going to be anything but *easy* for us sixty-somethings in his care. The exercise involves working your upper and lower body by lying on the floor on your back and rolling over. The trick, however, is that you must first "pretend" that you can use only your upper body (no helping whatsoever from your legs to roll you over) and then reverse it as if you have no use of your upper body (only your legs may participate now). We have had some marvelous laughs at one another practicing this at home!

This gave me warm resonance for our granddaughter Eloise, at four months old, as she worked ever so hard to roll over onto her tummy. Mind you, she has full use of arms and legs, but she also sports her beautiful large head, rolypoly tummy and her well-padded, cloth-diapered little bum. That is a lot to roll over! With determination and half-successes, she worked for days to accomplish the feat—ta da! But wait! Why was she starting to pucker her little lip and look on the verge of tears? Ahhh...it's one thing to roll over, yet it is another whole regimen to manage to roll back again! After a few days, she shifted her intentions from rolling over to pulling off her socks and putting her toes in her mouth—an equally satisfying bodily delight!

While watching her, my mind wandered to the early days of our first childcare center. In this heartwarming place we called "the new neighborhood," "the village" or simply "home away from home," we cared for small mixed-aged groups of children from four months to six years old. How could we be sure that the infants in our care were given a place of honor to perform their indefatigable acts of growing from supine to prone, then from quadruped to a fully upright participant of the "household?" We learned quickly that with family-sized groups, everyone—from toddlers all the way to the adults—was so keenly aware of the babies that there was nothing to really worry about. We delineated a protected space that was evident to all and experienced the glee of watching the sacred unfolding of the little ones in our care.

Never will I forget the day that toddler Ali "taught" newly upright Rhonda her next moves. Like a personal trainer, Ali stood in front of Rhonda demonstrating how to stand and squat repeatedly without falling. It was one of the most empathetic and endearing acts I have ever witnessed. And, as noted earlier, within days little Rhonda found her balance and took her first steps.

It was heartwarming also to realize that our premise was true, that a homelike environment provides all that children need. We did not have any specialized equipment; rather, we had couches, end tables, bookshelves and adult-sized chairs and dining table—in other words our childcare center looked like a group of apartments where people lived. Actually, we did

have one of those rocking boats
that can also turn over and be a
set of stairs which the toddlers
and preschoolers enjoyed occasionally.

Just like in a home, our infants were treasured. Each baby
had her or his own name song,
and at diapering time the other
children would often congregate near the changing site just to enjoy hearing the baby's song and watch the gestures of the little hands and feet.
All the children came to understand that when the baby started pulling
up, then some things on the shelves would have to be moved up and the
pretty cloth draping over our nature table would go away for a while. They
were aware when the caregiver was quietly rocking the baby or if it was
feeding time. Everyone became more tender. In fact, the tenderness was
translated into the children's behavior with their dolls, which were now
being gently swaddled, rocked, fed and pat-a-caked!

But what about the babies? How was it for them to be in a group of
mixed-age children? It is lovely to know that everyone else became more
gentle by having a baby around, but can we equally say it was rightful for
these "fresh-from-heaven" souls? Daily we observed how the infants' faces
would light up when one of the children drew near. They studied their older
"siblings" like human textbooks of their burgeoning selves. It was not only
the adults and the environment which were their curriculum; it was read-
ily the other children, as well.

As discussed in "Child as Curriculum," what was of utmost importance
was providing adequate space and time for the infants' self-discovery (usually only one infant in each "family unit"). Large areas were provided both
inside and outside for the infants to lie and gaze into infinite space. They
were never placed under a close-hanging bunch of jangling objects to keep
them mesmerized. Rather, one or two small objects would be placed nearby

on the floor to encourage their reach, eventually leading to rolling over. Outside they would lie on blankets surrounded by hay bales for protection, again allowing their gaze to extend as far as possible. There was no sense of hurry or rush when they needed to chew on their toes for a bit before having their socks put back on. Indeed, slowing things down was one of the greatest gifts bequeathed to all of us. And what was so clearly evident with the infants helped to remind us that in all of early childhood children need T-I-M-E to discover the world and play themselves in to their earthly existence.

3

Adult as Curriculum/ Child as Apprentice

For the small child before the change of teeth, the most important thing in education is the teacher's own being.

—RUDOLF STEINER, IN *ESSENTIALS OF EDUCATION*

The interesting word in this statement is the word *teacher*. Various caregivers feel differently about this word. Some feel it is too *school* oriented. Others feel it helps the children's parents feel better about where they are bringing their children, sensing that if you are a teacher, then their children are going to learn something. Some feel it is a title of respect. Others feel it is impersonal and not warm enough to express the type of care being provided. Some caregivers refer to themselves as "aunt" or "grandpa," as in an extended family. Whatever we call ourselves, it is essential to be aware that the children are learning about life through us, through our essential selves.

> The child is a perfect mimic; thus it is our task to make our-
> selves worthy of imitation. We ought to order our lives so that
> the child's perception can be immersed in him without hurt.
>
> —Rudolf Steiner, in *Understanding Young Children,*
> from the lecture series *The Child before the Seventh Year*

When founding a Waldorf school in North America in the late 1980s, the adults (parents, fellow teachers and staff) agreed that we were ALL "teachers" when in the presence of the young child. This was a bit surprising to some at first, when I asked all the adults to imagine themselves as teachers of the children. On the other hand, it offered a respectful awareness to the adults that while I was considered "the teacher," the children would also be influenced by all of them—observing how they interacted with each other in the hallway, how they dealt with finding a parking space, how they spoke about school politics. I told the story of my favorite teacher when I was a young child—not someone with the typical teacher tools, but rather someone with a broom, mop, hammer and nails. It was the school custodian, whose active and engaged life, gentle spirit and kind smile compelled me to seek him out whenever I had the opportunity.

Of course, parents also love to hear the stories of how we see their personal gestures in their children, just as they often tell us how they see us in their children when they are at home: "She always snuffs the candle in the exact same way I have seen you do it." Creating a community of imitable adults is such a gift for children. However, over time it becomes equally important to lead the adults in the understanding of the next phases of their children's lives, in which our hope and intention are that they become fully their individual selves, marked more by their eternal quest and calling than by the physical imprint of any of us. Still, that early imprint sets the stage for children's interface with the world and their own search for health and balance.

This begs the question: *How do we order our lives so the child's percep-*

tion can be immersed in him without hurt? A starting point might be to consider the word *perception*. Every encounter we have creates a perception. Think of the young child, freshly arrived on Earth, and how *everything* is new. Every sense impression leaves...well, it leaves an impression! So how do we order our lives, particularly during those times when we are with young children, in such a way that every sense impression can be safely penetrated by the children, who become their surroundings? Young children lack filters and merge with their impressions. Okay, right now pat your head and rub your tummy simultaneously. Remember that? It involves real concentration. A young child typically cannot achieve this, yet metaphorically the pace of our contemporary culture expects them to do this all the time! For a child's perception to become immersed in anything, it requires a slower pace and not too many things happening all at once. There are a growing number of *s-l-o-w* or *simplicity* organizations in our world now, Life-Ways being one of them. However, we don't really need to join one more thing. We simply need to be more consequent in our choices of activities and the pace with which we do them.

> What matters in the kindergarten is that the children should have a harmonious relation to those who are in charge of them and that these people should behave quite naturally, so that the children are naturally led to imitate them.
>
> —Rudolf Steiner, in *Understanding Young Children*

The journey to myself can be a lifelong journey for most of us. It was three years after being a "student teacher" before I started to flower into an authentic self—a self that flowers, fades, blossoms, wilts and needs reseeding throughout life. So a good question to ask is, "How can the children be in a harmonious relation to someone who is not yet in a harmonious relation to herself?" We do our best to honor, respect and recognize that we

are all in the human condition, all works in progress. It can be painful to read from Rudolf Steiner that our behavior can have a negative impact on a child's health when he enters middle age! Who among us does not remember a time when we lost our temper and spoke loudly or sharply to a child or group of children in our care? Yet, we are also told about the importance of striving and making amends. If we want our children to become resilient, we do well to model resilience (and self-forgiveness). While they may temporarily imitate our outbursts, they will also learn to imitate our strengths and our "overcomings." Of course, if one discovers that he or she is angry often, it may be time to change professions or take a sabbatical from being with young children. We can't really do that as parents, but we can send up a red flag, asking our community to help us. And as community members, we can be on the lookout for the overwhelmed parent who needs our extended hand rather than our criticism.

Another part of "behaving naturally" around the children can be revealed in how we interact with our colleagues and partners. In a homelike approach to care, we encourage the caregivers/teachers to communicate in the way good friends or neighbors would communicate, yet keeping the presence of the children in mind. In other words, we want to sustain the integrity of our best selves and, at the same time, relax and enjoy one another. Gentle humor among partners or colleagues can go a long way toward keeping life real in the most positive sense.

In our training we speak about the *Representative of Humanity*, a sculpture carved by Rudolf Steiner and others, at the Goetheanum (an architectural wonder in Switzerland that houses the organizational offices for international anthroposophical endeavors). As the central Human figure in the sculpture represents balance in life, it is surrounded by sclerotic figures of Ahriman, representing forces of materialism, and the "floating" figure of Lucifer, representing forces of ungroundedness. And in the corner above them all, one can see a small figure referred to as Cosmic Humor. Dr. Steiner held humor in high regard and, even though the way he speaks of humor reveals its higher calling, we can observe how the children delight when the adults in their midst share a laugh or a chuckle. Humor is known to repel negative energy, and levity has health-restoring properties.

Equal to humor, it is lovely for the children to see that adults around them have a sincere interest in one another's well-being and that they know how to problem-solve together. Just as in a home with parents, it is fine for the children to overhear how caregivers/teachers work through the plans for a festive meal or how to arrange a new piece of furniture.

We encourage natural conversation, not chattiness or gossip. And, above all, we encourage authenticity in the adults. Authenticity is not an invitation to adopt the mantra, "What you see is what you get" or "This is just who I am." Rather, our goal is to be who we are while striving to become our best selves. If we are in service to children and families, we expect our striving to include an ever-growing understanding of young children and, thus, an understanding of how our being affects them. More will be said about this in the section on Relationship-Based Care.

∞

> *How must I behave* becomes the question, in order that the child may attain to full possession of that consciousness of freedom which constitutes the dignity of man, and on which true happiness depends; how can I procure for him this highest good of earthly existence? And wherefore is it that I have been called to help and educate him?
>
> —Rudolf Steiner

It is easy to feel daunted by the weight and dignity asked of us when circumstances invite us into the life of a child or group of children. This is where trust reigns supreme. During the time Rudolf Steiner calls *the cosmic midnight hour,* when an individual, in league with cosmic forces, is laying out a path for incarnation, we can imagine that that individual's future encounter with us is part of his or her destiny plan. Sometimes it is helpful to consider that our encounter with that child (and all the children in our care) was also part of *our* pre-birth plan! To meditate upon and hold the question, "Why am I in this child's life?" is a deed of love. And when we partner with the child's guardian angel, we are partnering with the quintessential caregiver of that child's eternal self. One way we can help the child to "procure the good" is to be a living representative of the good, and the spiritual world will support us in that effort.

> In helping the child as he learns to walk, we must be pervaded by love; in helping the child to gain the power of speech, we must be absolutely truthful; and since the child is one great sense organ and in his inner physical functions also copies the spiritual, our own thinking must be clear if right thinking is to develop in the child from the forces of speech.
>
> —Rudolf Steiner, in *A Modern Art of Education*

We have discovered a helpful discussion in our training around this theme. How do we lovingly support the child as she or he is coming into the upright and then is refining this upright posture and movement? What does it mean to have an atmosphere of truthfulness as a child is coming into speech—truthfulness in ourselves and in the surrounding environment? How do we strengthen clarity of thought in ourselves as a child is awakening to thinking? Rather than share the many wonderful ideas that have come from these discussions, I encourage your own ponderings, particularly with a group of colleagues. You will be surprised at the range of awareness that will come to you, from the simple to the profound. Three short stories might help illustrate these principles:

Lovingly supporting movement. While still actively caregiving in our first childcare center, I daily observed a toddler, big for his age, fuss and beg to be put into our climbing tree as he watched the older, more capable children climb with delight. The temptation to offer him a boost was strong at times, particularly as he was extremely agile in his body. We all held ourselves back, however, and lovingly encouraged him that his time was coming. Unfortunately, I had to move to another state, but I happened to be visiting on the day that he achieved the climb on his own. Oh, the ecstasy! His joy was palpable, and the contentment and satisfaction that we felt as his loving caregivers was equally light-filled.

Truth in our speaking. When my youngest goddaughter was just coming into her speech and word acquisition, she and her mother and big sister came for a visit. While the girls and I were on a walk, the little one pointed to a plane flying overhead and said, "Cow!" Hmmm—interesting concept, but not quite accurate. When I mentioned this to her mother, she paused and then laughed, recalling that in the Chicago airport there was a sculpted cow hanging from the ceiling, and extended out from both sides of the cow were the real wings of a bi-plane. As a child pointing to everything she saw and asking, "What's dat?", her mother had answered, "Cow." How was she to know that the child was focusing on the wings? With no fault to the mother, the child's concept was wrongly formed (though easily corrected). In reality, however, the sculpture did not represent the truth of "cow" or "airplane." This does not mean the artist was wrong in his creation (it was art), but it does give us pause as we realize how children, each one a little *Adam* in the phase of naming the world, are trying to make sense of things. This is the best reason I can think of to delay putting technological images into the heads of children in early childhood—particularly those under the age of three. What a gift for them to experience "real" through their physical senses before they have to navigate "virtual"!

Clarity in our thinking. Watching a father with his two young children one evening in the library, I noticed how calm and secure these little ones seemed. As the toddler boy began to run, the father calmly said, "Walking." The boy and his slightly older sister proceeded to where they were going, took care of their business, and then, with a jaunt in their steps and a wave to the librarians, headed out the door with their father. Through the window I noticed that they had stopped and were looking up under the awning. The little girl was pointing something out to her brother, and when the father came to see, he gazed for some time as well. Though I could not hear them, I could see satisfaction on the children's faces as they were allowed to watch and wonder and tell each other what they were seeing before their father offered only a few words. When he ushered them to the car, he appeared to have a quiet confidence regarding when to hold the reins tight, when to let them out ever so slightly, when to offer explanations, and when to revel in the wonder.

This was a stark contrast to another event I observed when a young family was in line to order food and both parents turned to the four-year-old child to ask her what she wanted—this or that or the other thing or maybe that dish over there or.... As the child decided, changed her mind, decided again, fussed and seemed uncertain, the parents became frustrated and urged her to make up her mind. It ended with the child in tears and the family giving up their fun event and going home.

What an interesting phrase is "make up your mind." It is not unusual for our adult culture to be confused about how children learn to make up their minds. Surprisingly, it is not by giving them choices when they are young so they can exercise decision-making. Oddly, it is the opposite, most particularly with the young child. Remember that young children learn by imitating all that surrounds them. That includes imitating how we think and how we process things, not just what we do. The more clear-minded and decisive we are about what our children need, about what is going to happen in the course of the day and the week, and about the whether, what, how and when of things, the more we are modeling healthy thinking processes for the growing child to imitate. Even experiencing us "change our minds" thoughtfully and purposefully can exhibit creative thinking for them. It is not a matter of being rigid; it is a matter of clarity.

> When a child enters physical existence, he only continues the experiences he had in the spiritual world prior to conception. There we live, as human beings, within the beings of the higher hierarchies; we do what originates as impulses from the nature of the higher hierarchies. There we are imitators to a much higher degree because we are united with the beings we imitate. Then we are placed into the physical world. In it we continue our habit of being one with our surroundings. This habit extends to being one with, and imitating, the people around us who have to take care of a child's education by doing, thinking and feeling only what he may imitate.
>
> —Rudolf Steiner, in *Education as a Social Problem*

In this quote we seem to be moving into deeper and deeper (or higher and higher) spiritual terrain. If thinking beyond everyday existence, or perhaps beyond our childlike sense of God or a Greater Good, is somewhat new for you, then as a beloved colleague, Georg Kühlewind, used to say, "Fasten your seatbelts!" Rudolf Steiner offered us all a profound understanding of what it is to be an eternally unfolding being, cared for and in league with a multitude of other non-physical devoted Beings.

A great starting point to open our-selves to larger thinking could be to re-ally ponder a seed. If we wanted to be perfectly silly, we might try to take a plant and stuff it back into the seed from which it sprang. Okay, that didn't work. Yet, at one point, when that plant was mostly promise and possibility, its pre-existence was in that seed. In order for it to emerge, tending took place. That seed needed to experience a rela-tionship to soil, water, light and air (or combinations thereof) in order to become a plant or a tree. Spiritual science awakens the awareness that, as emerging spiritual beings, we humans, in our pre-existence, have also been and are being tended.

At this point, that understanding just makes me smile! But it didn't always. Stretching myself beyond my limited doctrinal upbringing to con-cepts that included a multitude of heavenly hosts with specific purposes and intentions—spiritual beings who, by the way, have a keen interest in how I handle this gorgeous gift called life—was a bit like trying to get my medium-sized body into a petite-sized pair of jeans! Not only was it awk-ward; it also just didn't fit! Becoming a partner, when I was 21, to some-one who read sentences to me such as "Our thoughts are food for the an-gels" and keeping a straight face while he was reading it, was my starting point toward a new way of thinking.

Further, becoming a mother, teacher, caregiver and grandmother sealed my fate! Being around these little seedlings we call babies and watching capacities emerge from them every moment, the evidence that they are held in a community of care beyond their human community is clear with every wobbly step, every emerging word, and every twinkled eye revealing awakening thought! Steiner indicates these little ones are imitating, in a physical way, the spiritual activity of the beings who cared for them before they were born! And now they are going to imitate me? Yikes! Did I really sign up for this? Is this going to be hard?

We have already acknowledged that we are imperfect beings. Yet, we do not want to fall prey to excusing ourselves from striving or, we might say, from our daily practice. In the realms of doing, thinking and feeling, we have been offered a wonderful series of exercises, sometimes referred to as Steiner's "Basic Exercises." When we work with them as an accompaniment to The Eightfold Path he describes, we place ourselves in a position of developing habits which can be positive models for the children in our care. Most importantly, these practices help us learn how to separate the essential from the non-essential, and in that way, we can trust that what we do in our daily lives is worthy of imitation.

While we may not recall our own time in the spiritual world in the direct care of the hierarchies, we can remember their individual gifts every time we watch the unfolding of a child from birth to three. As we observe the infant coming into the upright, developing the capacity for speech and becoming a being who thinks, we know these represent the child's deep imitation of these spiritual beings. We also learn from Dr. Steiner's research that the content of our thoughts are in service to the Archai; how we move, our gestures, serves the Archangels; and the substance of our speech is like food for the Angels. If we accept this as true, then we can see that in serving the needs of the child in the first three years by being persons of clarity, gracefulness and truthfulness, we are also serving our spiritual caretakers. It is like a full circle of care.

∞

> All human inquiry must proceed from wonder! That statement must be received in a perfectly positive way, my dear friends. In actual fact, in the soul that wants to penetrate to truth, this condition must first be present: The soul must stand before the universe in a mood of wonder and marveling.
>
> —Rudolf Steiner, in *Understanding Young Children*, from *The World of the Senses and the World of the Spirit*, Hanover, December 1911

Can you imagine any greater gift than spending days with young children, for whom almost every encounter is filled with wonder! In his lecture "Working with the Angels in the Astral Body of Man," Dr. Steiner mentions that miracles happen every single day—if only we have the senses to perceive them. It can be easy to miss the wonder if we are overwrought with concern about which story we are going to tell, when we will finish a craft project, how many meetings we have to attend at the end of the day, and the other content of our overwhelmed minds. Schedules and rhythms are important for the development of healthy breathing and purposeful activity. It helps us to remember, however, that not every wonderful thing we want to offer has to happen every day or even every week.

At LifeWays we have developed something we call "framing," which is a way to break down a daily and a weekly schedule so that one can see where the overwhelm starts to slip in. On behalf of the young child (and in truth, for us as well), the frame always starts with only food and sleep. It looks like this:

Sleep (or morning waking)
Food (breakfast)
Food (morning snack)
Food (midday meal)
Sleep (midday rest time)
Food (afternoon snack)
Food (evening meal)
Sleep (bedtime)

A few more sleep and food times are included if you are an infant! There may be times in our lives when sleep and food are all that we can manage: for example, if we have just given birth, if we are ill or depressed, or if we are in a big transition. For bodily survival, these two things are essential. However, our soul and spirit yearn for more. This is also true of the young child, who has come from heaven in order to get to know the earth. Sleeping and eating are just the beginning of the journey.

So what happens when we begin to fill in those spaces between the sleeping times and the eating times? We look at our *Living Arts Chart,* where we have listed every experience we value in the four categories of practical/domestic activity, nurturing care, creative exploration and social awareness. We determine which of the activities need to happen every day, which ones weekly, and which ones could be a little less frequent, perhaps monthly or seasonally. The ones we have deemed necessary to do every day now must be filled in between the sleeping and eating times, along with things on particular days that we feel must be done weekly:

Sleep/Waking

Items on your daily/weekly lists

Food

Items on your daily/weekly lists

Food

Items on your daily/weekly lists

Food

Items on your daily/weekly lists

Sleep/Rest

Items on your daily/weekly lists

Food

Items on your daily/weekly lists

Food

Items on your daily/weekly lists

Sleep

The choices we make for where to place these activities will have a direct impact on the quality of the eating experiences and the depth of the restfulness. They will also have a serious impact on whether we have left enough room for *wonder, discovery and joy*.

By choosing home life as the model for our daily experience with the children, we are less inclined to over-program the day. Food preparation, tending the household and garden, and nurturing the bodily care of the children and ourselves provide a full menu of meaningful activities and intentions for the children to imitate. Weaving stories or nursery rhymes, games and music into the course of the week offers levity to all of the other purposeful work being done.

Levity or leaven also comes in when the caregiver/teacher learns to place value on creating a personal life that is fulfilling—full and filling. *Full* does not have to do with measurement (having or doing a lot of things), but rather having a sense of meaning-full-ness in life. *Filling* has to do with a sense of satisfaction. There is a Zen quote we work with that encourages us to make little distinction between our work and our play. In fact, in creating their daily, weekly, and seasonal life charts, the caregivers/teachers/parents are encouraged to include their whole life on the chart, not only a schedule of the time they are with the children in their care. We encourage the possibility to see the relationship of "work" life to "personal" life so the two actually begin to flow in and through one another. In this way we can become more and more authentic in ourselves. We are not a caregiver persona when we are with the children and a different persona when we are away from them. Even though some of the adult things we do on our own are not things we would do with young children (e.g., go to an adult movie or sit for a half hour in silent meditation), we can begin to recognize them as part of what supports the *wonder* in our lives. When we feel *wonder*ful, when we have nourished our formative forces with health-giving experiences, we can continue in our work with young children for longer stretches of time.

Relationship-based Care

As regards all of the quotes in this section, it should be noted that the term "relationship-based" care is the foundational principle upon which our approach to care and education is built! It is the scaffolding upon which all other ideals and intentions rest.

Recently re-reading an interview with Dr. Helmut von Kügelgen, the late director of the International Association of Steiner/Waldorf Early Childhood Education, I was reminded of how deep this relationship runs. As has been noted, these tiny individualities come to us directly from Spirit in order to work on yet another chapter of living and learning on Earth. We understand that we are the guides/mentors/examples-of-life upon which they begin to build their greater understanding of how things work. Dr. von Kügelgen reminds us that is not singularly based on our outer deeds and decisions but includes how we think and feel about things as well.

This brings to mind a verse in the poem, *Thus a Child Learns*, by Frederick J. Moffitt:

> *Day by day, the child comes*
> *to know a little bit of what you know;*
> *to think a little bit of what you think;*
> *to understand your understanding.*

Dr. von Kügelgen pointed out that how we understand the larger context of what it is *to be* directly affects the child's sensibilities about it. If we speak or teach or offer a child a prayer that includes the concept of a guardian angel, yet we do not actually believe in such beings, this may have a negative effect on the child. Perhaps a more common example can be found in how we bring such concepts as Saint Nicholas or the Tooth Fairy. When we understand a higher truth behind the existence of these beings, the child can actually bear learning, when they are older, that we participated in the gifting inspired by such beings.

How well I remember walking through Ashdown Forest with my elder son when he was nine and being asked the question, "Are you the Tooth

Fairy?" While an initial sadness came over me that he was truly leaving behind early childhood, I also experienced relief that I could answer him from my own relationship to, and appreciation of, elemental beings. To be able to offer a brief historical perspective on human beings' relationship to the fairy kingdom felt like a gift. I explained how things had changed from a time when folk actually left food and drink out for the farm's wee folk in the evenings to current times when modern people tended not to believe in these beings, thus creating a withdrawal of their presence in our daily lives. I could share stories of how his Papa worked with nature spirits to help grow our garden. I could speak of the interest fairy folk have in teeth, those little miracles of individuality that make us visible to them, thus the folk lore of the Tooth Fairy coming to collect the teeth. To be able, with honesty, to say that Papa and I chose the gifts from the Tooth Fairy out of our wish to partner with the fairies seemed to make sense to our son. He was not bereft; in fact, he immediately said, "And how about Saint Nicholas?" Admittedly, it was nice to be in a forest setting (Winnie the Pooh's "Hundred Acre Wood" to be exact) when these questions were posed!

Rather than furthering concepts with our children that hold no sense of truth for us, Dr. von Kügelgen encourages our own depth of exploration regarding the visible and invisible worlds we inhabit. Thus we can bring our own truth to the children in our care and not set up in them a lack of trust or belief. A sense of wonder, of mystery and magic, can be like manna to the young child when the adult bringing the stories is open to such mysteries. And, as these children grow into adulthood, it is a gift to have a foundation from which to spring regarding their own sensibilities about spiritual beings who support them. They may or may not use the same language or concepts that you offered them in childhood.

A favorite modern troubadour, Fred Rogers, offered his own brand of mystery and make-believe through a most odd medium of our times, the television. The screen was his venue to reach millions of children daily; one could even imagine it as his "pulpit" for bringing spirit-lifting content to the little ones. Perhaps he is the one person who, through his integrity and higher sense of purpose, actually transcended the deleterious effects we understand that screens can have on children. As regards relationship-based care, Mister Rogers said:

> *My hunch is that if we allow ourselves to give*
> *who we really are to the children in our care,*
> *we will in some way inspire cartwheels in their hearts.*

This may not always look like the examples above, where we are offering specific content to our children through dialogue. How we move in the world, how we concentrate on matters at hand, how we encounter our fellow beings—all of these leave an imprint on our children. From *The Tender Land* by Kathleen Finneran comes an example of how gesture and intention have an effect on a child observing her mother: "As a child, whenever I saw her sitting at the kitchen table with the bills spread out around her, I knew I could sit right next to her and never be noticed. Instead of being bothered by her inattention, I felt calmed by it. Sitting beside her, unacknowledged, I felt as if I were in some special zone, a quiet, impenetrable place she had created with her concentration.... And so I sat beside her, happy to be enveloped in her disregard, the suspension of time that came with it.... Did she know how soothing she could be, how she could shrink the world down to this for me?"

We can see from this example that we are not talking about "putting on" some cloak (or apron) of "otherliness" that is not quite true to who we are but somehow represents who we think we are supposed to be. Striving always toward our best selves is a worthy goal and one worthy of our children's observing. Let's be honest that we are in a constant state of growth and development regarding who we are and what we believe in. This, we could say along with Mister Rogers, is *who we really are*. It is not a matter of speaking to little children about our personal development, about our doubts and wonderings. Rather it is essential that we develop our own understanding of the bigger venue, the vast and broad world of spiritual/physical being that encompasses all of us, so that what we represent to the young child through our personal self is authentic, even while we are in our own state of growth.

Perhaps another, more subtle, way to interpret relationship-based care has to do with our understanding that the young child feels a relationship to every thing and every one he or she encounters. While we can truthfully imagine ourselves to be a major part of the young child's curriculum of life, so is everyone else. In this regard, we have come to appreciate mixed-age care, which offers some surprising benefits to both the children and the caregivers.

One unexpected advantage of mixed-age groups was brought home to me years ago when I attended a huge childcare convention and thought, "I wonder what the topic is of that workshop?" It was a large hall that seated at least five hundred, and people were spilling out into the hallway. Naturally I was drawn in. It must be important, I thought. The speaker was already engaging with the audience when I slipped in to the back of the room and heard her acknowledging their lamentation of dealing every day with toddlers biting other toddlers. That was the theme of the workshop— "biting." Yes, I recognize this as an honest concern for caregivers, particularly since it is one of the things most upsetting to parents. We had certainly experienced it in our own care centers and homes; however, it was typically short-lived and recognized as a developmental stage that could be supported creatively for the individual child.

It was different for us, however, because we typically had only one to two biters to deal with at a time in any given mixed-age group. And with older children in the mix, the time period for dealing with a biter was shortened even more. Older children usually let a toddler know quickly and clearly that biting is NOT OK! Toddlers desire to be accepted by older children and will often change their behavior accordingly. In addition to skilled caregivers' knowing how best to support a biter, being in a mixed-age, family-size group also mitigated much of the problem. Even in groups of up to twelve children, when the ages are mixed it is an extremely different experience from the typical toddler room in conventional care settings. I listened sadly as one caregiver after another in the packed workshop shared

stories of tending to multiple biters in their rooms filled only with toddlers and/or two-year-olds. It seems that the closest we might come to that experience in a real live home would be when sextuplets are all teething at the same time!

Multi-age care settings not only offer caregivers the support of the slightly older children, but also provide the children glimpses of "before and after." Imagine the delight of watching 12-month-old Rhonda observing 18-month-old Ali one day as she lowered herself from a standing to a squatting position over and over again. Rhonda was on the verge of standing up and stepping out into the world, yet still had hesitancy. With such tenderness, Ali seemed to be demonstrating to Rhonda, "You can do it; see, it looks like this!" Equally beautiful is the gaze of a four-year-old absorbed in the wonder of the kicks and squeals of the infant being diapered or lying next to a new crawler on the floor. There is a perfect wholeness to the early childhood years. Yet when we put children into compartmentalized age groupings, a sense for the continuity of the unfolding disappears. It is as if we start specialization earlier and earlier.

The fundamental principle of attachment also suffers under the single-age model. It seems no accident when children are born into the same family. When they need to be cared for outside of the family, there is something rightful about being able to stay together. Siblings, it seems, have chosen that relationship for a reason. Sometimes one senses a closeness that is palpable. Other times it seems they have come to rub off each other's rough edges! Their rough and tumble play can be one way this is exhibited. When they are in full-day care, the opportunity to spend that time together is shortened if they have to be sent to separate age groupings for the full day. For children who are the only child in their family, a different benefit becomes apparent. One senses that they acquire non-blood siblings and, thus, are also allowed to experience the fullness of the unfolding ages. Many parents have told us that when their firstborn spent time in our care with infants and toddlers in the mix, they seemed more prepared to accept their new sibling when a second child came along. They already had a sense for the commitment involved in the care of babies.

What seems most obvious regarding relationship-based care is the importance of bonding to one's caregivers throughout the course of early childhood. Both common sense and research support the importance for a child of not changing caregivers as often as it happens in childcare settings today. A well bonded child is one who has come to know/love and be known/loved by one or a few caregivers over a period of years. In fact, the safety and warmth a child experiences in healthy, long-term relationships is often cited as a great predictor of that child's brain development, sense of self-worth, social ability, and even future income bracket! This is not because the child bonded to perfect people (shhh—don't tell anybody, but there aren't any), but because, in all their imperfections, a person or small group of people provided constancy, interest, love and lives worthy of imitating to the child.

In most large, conventional care settings, young children may have as many as ten different caregivers by the time they are two or three. This may not be by design, but in a culture where caring for our most vulnerable and innocent citizens is not valued through recognition or income, it is difficult to retain caregivers for long-term employment. On the other hand, most care settings (and many licensing regulations) are designed to change the child's caregivers regularly. It is not unusual for a child to move from an infant room to a toddler or twos room, to preschool, to pre-K, to kindergarten—all by the time the child is five. Even in some private schools that offer extended care, a young child may have several primary caregivers/teachers in one day: arriving early to be cared for by the early-care person, then attending the main program (whether it be nursery, pre-K or K), followed by the aftercare person, and finally the late-afternoon person.

How can our culture keep doing this when we have learned so much about how children thrive in care based on bonding, simplicity and a sense of feeling at home in their environment?

To avoid being too bleak, it is important to acknowledge the resiliency and grace that surround the young child. However, what a gift it is when we offer them care based on wholeness, bonding, familiarity and predictability. Life always brings us to brinks where we need grace and resiliency to wrap around us. We want our care settings, however, to be havens of protection and connection, rather than being part of the model of overwhelm so many young children must navigate today.

Ponderables

⚭ So, how *do* you order your life so that a young child's perception can be immersed in it without hurt, without becoming overwhelmed?

⚭ Think of one thing that, with some effort, you could do less in order to afford more time for activity worthy of imitation by young children. For example, could you participate in social networking three times a week instead of every day, or for half an hour every day instead of two hours?

⚭ Create a list of everything you can think of in the four *Living Arts* categories that matters in your life (practical, nurturing, creative and social activities). Now, categorize those things into *daily, weekly, monthly* and *seasonal* or *as needed* categories.

⚭ Create a weekly chart with days of the week across the top and half-hour time slots down the side and fill in everything on your *Living Arts* list. LifeWays students work with their charts throughout the months of their training, refining and re-defining *what truly matters*. Over time, one does not need to be so prescriptive as to have half-hour time slots measuring life. It is simply a tool to help us initially get a grip on what it is that we actually do and what we honestly want to do.

⚭ List from one to three habits you have that you feel are beneath your dignity—they do not represent your highest and best self, and you would not want children to imitate them. Now write a brief plan for overcoming one of these habits, including a timeline.

⑥ List three of your best qualities and try to imagine or remember how these developed in you. If you can trace them back to someone who made an impression on you or a life situation that crafted these qualities in you, quietly give thanks for that person or those events.

⑥ List something about a colleague or partner that is difficult for you to work with while caring for children. Reflect on how you might help to improve the situation and include finding a way to appropriately share your concern. Be open to hearing that person's concerns about you as well. When possible, make a plan together to support each other in personal growth and development.

⑥ List three things about a colleague or partner that are worthy of being imitated by young children. When possible, share these with that person.

⑥ Pause. Reflect. Imagine the children in your care seeking you as part of their life plan.

⑥ How do we lovingly support the child as he or she is coming into the upright and then refining this upright posture and activities?

⑥ What does it mean to have an atmosphere of truthfulness—in ourselves and in the surrounding environment—as a child is coming into speech?

⑥ How do we strengthen clarity of thought in ourselves as a child is awakening to thinking?

⑥ List the challenges you have encountered in your mixed-age early childhood program or home and spend the next three weeks finding creative ways to mitigate those challenges. Ask for help.

⑥ If you have mixed ages, list three of your favorite experiences. When possible, write about these and share with other caregivers/teachers.

4

Environment as Curriculum

The objects used in the kindergarten should be taken from actual life;
they should not be invented by an intellectual civilization.

—RUDOLF STEINER, IN *HANDWORK AND HANDICRAFTS,
INDICATIONS FROM RUDOLF STEINER*, BY HEDWIG HAUCK

Samuel, our grandson, at eight months old was pulling himself up on his
daddy's leg. Then it was the coffee table, then his bed. Our son, through
FaceTime on his phone, was sharing with us the experience of trying to
lower Sam's mattress so that he would not fall out of his bed now that he
was entering the upright! He referred to Sam as a "speed crawler," and I observed as he crawled over his brother that fellow human beings and typical household furniture seemed to provide him all that he needed for a
boost now and then.

There was a time that the idea of specialized equipment for infants
was unheard of. Perhaps there was a dream of having something like a
playpen, but I believe that such things were improvised. For developmental milestones to be achieved, the furnishings of daily life sufficed. Outdoor

spaces provided much of the up and down, in and out, under and over experiences. To observe this, watch the movie *Babies,* and you will see that the child with the most brilliant body knowledge and balance is the one who lived with the least material goods.

Whether driven by clever merchandising or the desire for accelerated development, equipment—a wide variety of equipment—hit the scene of babyland in recent decades. The variety of "necessities" on the market now is astonishing, not only for a baby coming into a family, but especially for infants and toddlers in childcare. In fact, one reason children are separated by age in many childcare settings is because of the idea that children, at every stage of development, need specific equipment, toys and educational materials for healthy development. The thought exists that to mix the ages is unfair to the children, inappropriate and, in fact, dangerous!

In our care settings, we have experienced an opposite phenomenon: Having family-sized groups of mixed ages typically creates an added layer of protection around the youngest. Not only are the caregivers watching carefully over the infant, but the older children are also paying close attention. An extra measure of care is given to protect the littlest ones from the general "traffic pattern" of the older children. For example, a quilt on the ground surrounded by hay bales might be set up outside as a clear indication to the active children that the baby is there. Care is taken that tiny play materials for the older children (such as acorns or corn or small blocks of wood) are tucked away on a shelf that is not accessible to the youngest toddlers. This is no different from how it is in a home with children in different stages of development. Slight adjustments are made according to the needs of the youngest child.

On the other hand, we also protect the social needs of the older children. A fond memory from our first LifeWays Center comes to mind. One of our families got a new refrigerator and, blessedly, remembered to save the packing box and bring it to us. Rosie and her friend, another four-year-old girl, immediately laid claim to the box and spent much dedicated time crafting it into a playhouse, even cutting a hole in the top and taping a silk over it for a skylight. We caregivers were committed to giving those girls ample time to play in the box without threat of everything being destroyed by the toddlers. It required a bit of extra attentiveness, but it was a wonderful life experience for all the children. The girls had delightful imaginative play, and the younger children experienced that the world did not end when a boundary was enforced and they were directed to other play areas.

Taking care that all of the children spend a good portion of each day outdoors insures that they will receive healthy stimuli for their bodily senses, particularly balance and self-movement or, as it is popular to call them now, vestibular and proprioception. This removes the need for the indoor environment to have equipment rather than furniture, which helps to make it feel more like home.

Home furnishings make wonderful play spaces. Rather than purchase play stands for our home-based parent-child program, my husband and I turned two of our overstuffed chairs back-to-back and created a playhouse with sheets and play cloths. An old coffee table with a few small chairs was just right for playing kitchen and restaurant. A small nook area was created by the placement of a chest of drawers near my wooden file cabinet. This is where the dollies live at my house, and when children visit, it is still an intimate corner for quiet play. And it takes only a moment to turn a dining table into a sizeable fort by tossing a large sheet over it. Musical instruments reside inside a cabinet in the living room, and a few special toys are kept on the lowest shelf of our bookcase.

Not every childcare site can achieve a full measure of home furnishings, but every effort is made to de-institutionalize the space. This is important not only for the children, but also for the caregivers/teachers. The more homelike the environment, the more natural it is for the adults to take up the tasks and necessities of a home. There is less inclination to become program-driven or equipment dependent. Having home as the model encourages things such as lamplight, rather than overhead lighting; chests of drawers, rather than cubicles; normal furniture, rather than everything child-size; and using high shelves where the adults can put a few things

that represent their lives (their knitting or mending basket, for example, or a favorite book of poems and verses, or special hand lotion). It is essential to understand that the adults who care for children are also "living" in the spaces we create. Environments that are set up to accommodate only children are strange to begin with, and one could also ask: What is the message this sends to the children? While giving a presentation on environments at a conference of the National Association for the Education of Young Children, I said to the participants, "So, when you awoke this morning to your house, lit up entirely by fluorescent track lighting, and sat at your child-sized table for breakfast, did you also enjoy all the posters, children's drawings, and alphabet covering almost every surface of the walls and the multiple things hanging from the ceiling?" The question seemed to stun the audience. Then I posed the question, "If this does not fit the description of 'home' to you, then why are you and the children in your care spending your days and weeks in such surroundings?"

We hope that the children in our care will be resilient and joyful, living in the experience of adults who are taking care of the natural tasks of home life while they, the children, are taking care of the natural tasks of childhood! This is less difficult to achieve in places that look, smell, feel and act like a home. Environments with specialized equipment or settings that are almost exclusively child-oriented are not necessarily wrong or misguided, particularly if the children are there only for short periods of time. When, however, the children are spending large portions of their daily and weekly lives in care settings other than their family home, they thrive in environments that provide the simple and practical experiences of daily living. This is also true for the adults providing the care.

The nurturing care so needed by children today is also well-served by a homelike environment. A couch or oversized chair offers enough room to play pat-a-cake with a baby on your lap while a toddler or four-year-old in need of cuddle time tucks in nearby. Two of my favorite couch experiences were in Wisconsin, where the children all sat in a row on the couch waiting their turn for a warm lavender foot bath, and in Colorado, where a soft blanket snuggly tucked in seven one- to five-year-olds on their couch every day for story time.

One further element needs to be considered in relation to environments. In government-regulated childcare, "safety" and "health" are the two main concerns of the regulatory bodies. There is a very interesting chapter in the book *Home Away from Home* regarding this topic. It encourages us to take a deeper look at how we interpret health and safety. A pristine, soft, no-risk environment may convey "safety" to some, but we might ask the question, "What about soul safety?" How is it for the child not to be allowed to test his bodily awareness or learn how to fall and maneuver back up again or to gain bodily strength and immunity by working through occasional illness? We must be sensible and not cavalier, not leave broken things lying around or an open staircase for a curious toddler to climb too far (rather, try putting the gate one or two steps up so he or she can practice without getting seriously injured by a fall). However, we also want to learn how to advocate with the regulators and inspectors, engaging them in meaningful conversation about the letter of the law as compared to the spirit of the law, encouraging open dialogue about the difference between relative-risk as compared to no-risk environments.

Much more could be written about "actual life" environments, but perhaps it is important to note that not all homes are the same and not all cultures are the same. What we are seeking is environments that are natural rather than clever, welcoming rather than compelling, and simple rather than contrived.

> **The joy of children in and with their environment must therefore be counted among the forces that build and shape the physical organs.**
>
> —Rudolf Steiner, in *The Kingdom of Childhood*

When I walked into the large, warehouse-like building that housed the birthday party of my four-year-old great-nephew, I could hear the screams and shouts of the children long before I arrived in the place they occupied. The variety and nature of the large-motor playscapes scattered throughout the space created a sort of frenzied behavior in the children. Were they having fun? They said that they were. Were they experiencing joy? That is not what I sensed.

There is a subtlety to joy that is difficult to describe. Perhaps it has more to do with self-discovery, spirited encounter, warm exchange with others, and time and space to digest what has been experienced. Children are well supported by environments that invite but do not overwhelm, that are open but can also be closed, that challenge but also comfort. Like cats, children typically love to be enclosed—for example in a box or under a table or be-

hind a desk or swaddled in a pram in infancy. Yet, they also like to expand—
for example, climbing a tree, rolling down a hill, running through an open
space, or lying on the floor to practice rolling over in infancy.

Some sensitive children may even imitate the gesture of the toys in
their environment. It is almost always safe to err on the side of simplicity
when it comes to the materials we provide. What can be more complex is
the variety of activities children experience the adults doing—laundry,
cooking, cleaning, mending, planning, gardening, tending to a vehicle, offering a puppet show, playing a game with the baby, and so on. When the
environment supports these kinds of activities for the adults, it also provides a meaningful environment for the children to imitate. This, coupled
with a daily rhythm that breathes easily, supports the opportunity for deep
play, which is a wonderful component of joy.

Rather than feeling daunted by the idea that the environments we create for the children can affect the healthy development of their organs, let us focus on an exercise showing what that might look like. What, for example, might a healthy rhythmic system (heart and lungs) need? The answer is inherent in the word *rhythmic,* isn't it? What happens to you when you feel overwhelmed? Perhaps you become a little short of breath, maybe even feel a little tightness in your chest. How can the environment we set up for young children be rich enough to encourage self-discovery and scarce enough to allow the development of deep connection? Scarcity (of "stuff," not of necessities such as food and shelter) is almost always more advantageous for healthy rhythms. There is an energy connected to "things," and we find ourselves feeling compelled to interact with that energy. Young children best develop healthy rhythmic organs when they can repeatedly manipulate the same things for weeks, months and sometimes years. If we know that providing this literally supports healthy hearts and lungs, it makes it easier to simplify our environments.

Certainly, we can say the same thing for the organs connected with our nerve-sense system. Have you experienced places that made you feel calm almost as soon as you walked in, as compared to other places that gave you a bit of a nervous twitter? What were some of the elements in those spaces? The brain of the young child is eager to apprehend the world, yet it also wants to be able to assimilate the various experiences into its actual physical make-up. Rather than "more" as a goal for the stimulation of babies' brains, how about the repetition of "same"? An environment that encourages repeated encounters not only supports synaptic connections in the brain but also helps to myelinate those pathways. Feeling "at home" in an environment can also be calming for the adult. A physical culture that is easy to deal with and is artistically pleasing to the adult can also support the young child. As long as we adults think things through in such a way that the children can become involved in our life activities if they wish, then we can be perfectly comfortable in creating life environments that support our practical and artistic needs as well as those of the children.

A further consideration in relation to the children's joy in the environment has to do with how well we integrate them into the creation of the environment. When we opened our first center, we were still renovating some of the rooms. The first children to come to us saw and heard the big equipment and the workers changing the structure, laying carpet and painting the walls. We also decided not to create the large, meandering sandbox before children were enrolled. Instead we spent nine months (some of them snowy winter months when we were unable to do much) digging and preparing the space in the back garden area. At last when the sand was delivered in the spring, we chose to have it poured outside of the gate so we could bring it in one wheelbarrow load at a time over the next two weeks. Oh, how those children loved those wheelbarrow rides! The children, the parents in the parent-child playgroup, and the first group of adult students in our training course all felt a kinship to that sandbox due to their personal participation in its creation. Even the infants experienced that it had happened in their presence. One side benefit of this was the expansion of our community to include the workers and craftspeople who also got to know the children. One gruff building contractor, who proclaimed, "Bah humbug!" when something involved "little kids," softened into a quiet-spoken, kind-eyed "uncle" who would often call and ask, "Do you need anything done this week?"

> **During the first period of life, the child's surroundings should be such that he may be assimilated by means of the senses, for, as we have explained before, the child imitates all that goes on in its surroundings in a bodily-religious way.**
>
> —Rudolf Steiner, in *Understanding Young Children*, quoted from *Walking, Speaking, Thinking—Imitation in a Bodily-Religious Way*, 1923

We already know this quote to be true; however, it behooves us to remind ourselves always of the child's natural devotion to whatever he or

she encounters. We do not mean the kind of devotion a lover feels for her sweetheart, which is often colored with feelings and perhaps even some sentimentality. The bodily-religious devotion the young child experiences toward her surroundings is of the same nature as the oneness she experienced prior to incarnation, while cradled in the non-material spiritual world. One can see in the infant's long gaze, in the toddler's caress, and in the two-year-old's lively dialogue over and through all surrounding sounds and noises, that the choices we make regarding the sights, sounds, touches, tastes, smells, thoughts, feelings and things that the child encounters will, in some way, merge into the child's being. This will be especially true, we know from neurological science, for those things and experiences that are regularly repeated.

For this reason, we take special care when "framing" the daily schedule and give close attention to those activities and things that will be a part of each routine. By starting, as described above, with sleep and food, we know we are covering the absolute necessities for the physical body. What we choose to do before and after the sleeping and eating helps to determine the quality of the experience. Jaimmie, the caregiver who created the DVD on sleep time, even discovered that for her children, the mood of the toothbrushing song she sang before naptime affected whether they entered nap restfully or nervously. The fun song she had been using served to bring delight and enjoyment, but also stirred the children. When she changed to a quiet, mood-of-the-fifth song, it made a difference in how the children settled into naptime.

As we grow in our understanding of the many facets of life, we can work ever more subtly with our choices. We may come to understand what sorts of activities work best in the hours before noon and which ones lend themselves more to the mood and nature of the air and the light after midday. We will discover that some schedules that worked well in one season when the days were long may need some shifts and changes during another season when daylight is more scarce or the air is more brisk. It is not just a matter of changing clothing for the season, but changing awareness of what qualities of life and death, light and dark, outer and inner accompany each season.

Ponderables

⑥ List three things you could do to make your care environment more homelike.

⑥ If you are using equipment in your program, what equipment can you imagine replacing with furniture instead? Or what equipment would be unnecessary if you took the children outside more often to experience the variety of movement offered there?

⑥ How can the environment we set up for young children be rich enough to encourage self-discovery and scarce enough to allow the development of deep connection?

⑥ Does your care environment reflect your interests and needs? If not, list three things you could change so that the environment appropriately and warmly accommodates you.

A Word about Advocacy

Most of us know many wonderful people who care for young children. They may find themselves caught in a system that, due to government regulation, administrative greed, overriding materialism, or simple ignorance, does not work out of an understanding of the fundamentals of physical and social/emotional health for young children.

Due to the resiliency of children, we often do not see the full results of the overwhelm we create for them until they are older. Or we are also too overwhelmed to try to stem the tide of what we know to be a growing tsunami of emotionally distant, restless, stressed and over-tired souls. Whether this description fits a caregiver at the end of the day or a child after years of emotionally detached care, if we are aware of it, what can we do about it?

There is a childcare center in Milwaukee, Wisconsin, where the children play outside every day—for long stretches of time—in all kinds of weather. Getting dressed and un-dressed in the winter is a major part of the "curriculum," and seasoned caregivers recognize the vast amounts of learning going on! These children eat whole foods, mostly organic and a lot homegrown, cooked before their eyes and smelled with their little noses, every day. Their toys are few, but lovely and open-ended. Their primary caregivers, along with their parents, have shown up, smiled at them, laughed with them, cleaned them, bejeweled them with music, stories, and art projects, said "no" to them when necessary, and offered them guidance and direction almost every day of their lives for years. Together they have celebrated birthdays, seasonal festivals, crossings and thresholds, first steps, first pearly teeth, potty successes, sunshine cracking open a cloud, icicles and frosted breath, treasures yielded by the forest floor, growing up with multi-colored friends and families, sad good-byes, giggly hellos, and a general sense of health and well-being. As a matter of fact, this center has one of the best reputations in the city.

But the implementation of a statewide childcare rating system has awarded this center only three stars on a scale of five. Parents keep telling their stories of how well their children are navigating life and school after they have outgrown the center and gone on to kindergarten or elementary school. Staff turnover is extremely low because of the respect, admiration and depth of relationship the caregivers experience there. Children continue to be on the high end of healthy as compared to many other settings. The enrollment wait list continues to be long. Goodness continues to manifest there every day. The beat, as they say, goes on. They may be rated three stars, but they are shining bright!

How does this kind of rating happen? In the state of Wisconsin, and in a growing number of states across the continent, quality rating systems are being employed that focus on materialistic measurables, such as the number of toys available to children, the amount of "stuff" hanging on the walls in the room, and the quantity and quality of the paper trail that accompanies every activity engaged in by caregivers, children and administrators. Playing outdoors every day, running down forest paths and eating organic whole foods cooked from scratch are not valued by the rating system.

The staff at this childcare center have chosen to remain in the rating system so they can continue to serve low-income children whose parents receive state subsidies for childcare. However, they have decided that they are willing to lose points for those things that are not necessary or appropriate for the quality of life they are providing the children in their care. They do not need, for example, to put sand tables in each of their rooms when the children are outside playing in a forest or in their very large outdoor sandbox every day. They do not need to overwhelm the children with print materials throughout their cozy home-like rooms when they are learning to navigate words very well through their exposure to music, stories, puppet shows, games and creative arts. They do not need to implement guided exercise programs designed to increase the children's heart rates to an acceptable level defined by regulators when the children have ample time to play freely in nature. What do they need? To stand in the integrity of knowing that what they are offering these children and families is a model of sustainable, simplicity-based living that has been proven repeatedly to engender healthy human beings.

Can you imagine yourself—as a parent, caregiver, teacher, nanny, grandparent or other person who cares about children and the future—speaking to people who are responsible for regulations and evaluation systems about the possibility of pushing a reset button, one based on healthy childhood? Can you imagine entering a respectful dialogue that doesn't necessarily point fingers of wrongdoing or backward thinking regarding current educational theory and practice, but rather requests an opening of minds and hearts to allow well-grounded and principled care practices to stand in the world via a different standard or evaluation system?

Many years ago when our oldest son had a car accident, I remember standing in the auto repair shop with him and listening as the young and capable repair person described all that needed to be done. When he went behind the counter to tally the cost, our son approached the counter, clearly weary from the day's events and with anticipation of the news he was about to receive. What happened next has been a constant reminder to me of what humanitarianism looks like. As the young mechanic looked across the counter, he paused before handing over the bill, then reached under the counter and brought out a bowl of fruit. "Would you like some fruit?" he offered. Momentarily stunned, our son let out a sigh (probably his first deep breath since the accident). "Yes, I could use a banana." Maybe you just had to be there in order to experience the sincerity behind the gesture. But in that moment, I thought, "This is what we want to see happen as a result of the care and education we offer children as they grow up." It was essential that this young man knew his trade, and indeed he was excellent in his work. Perhaps more important, however, was that he had the ability to perceive a suffering human being standing before him and had the wherewithal to extend the warmth of human kindness as well.

Early childhood is that ripe and rosy time when, fresh from heaven's light, children arrive open and trusting that what we bring them will represent the goodness of the world. It is a time for long pauses, quiet and rowdy play, touching, tasting, smelling and rolling around in everything, and for experiencing striving adults who, while still growing up themselves, are eager to find some semblance of joy in life. It is a time to feel "home" as a quality of experience as much as a place. It is a time for growing secure and safe and loved. Later, when physical and thinking capacities are ready for direct instruction and specialized talents to emerge, that is when we hope to encounter teachers schooled in specific skills. Then, perhaps, one day, the child who is allowed a delicious fiery, watery, airy, earthy early childhood and later comes under the tutelage of skill-based teachers, will be able to look up and see beyond the moment into the eternity of being.

In Conclusion

We feel an amazed debt of gratitude to Rudolf Steiner for sharing his insights gained through the awakening of spiritual science. We also find inspiration in the practical and researched understanding of child development from a variety of time-honored experts and pedagogues who have corroborated and extended Steiner's indications. However, Rudolf Steiner's awareness of the eternal intersection between the heavenly and the earthly, the vertical and horizontal gestures of life, and the sanctity of the child—in the first three years, in particular, and throughout early childhood—stand as a testament and deep calling to all we strive to develop in our care and education of these young souls.

Thus we return to the question posed earlier: "If we are caring for children, particularly very young children, all day long, are we providing an environment and activities that truly look and feel like home?" We offer a final list of *ponderables* for you to consider.

Ponderables

⚭ In your care environment are there homelike furnishings?

⚭ Do you have nooks and crannies for quiet, personal time? Open space for group play?

⚭ Is your outdoor environment safe, yet also inviting of wonder and adventure?

⚭ Are there opportunities for the children to experience adults engaged in household tasks such as meal preparation, laundry, cleaning, creating things for the *home*, sorting and repairing, gardening and such?

๑ Do the group sizes emulate a family experience more than a program experience?

๑ If, for some regulatory or financial reason, these things do not seem possible, are you advocating on behalf of the children for that to change? Are you willing to dialogue with regulatory agents about regulations that no longer represent the best interests of the children?

๑ Can you explain how and why you do the things that may seem questionable to regulatory agencies, helping them understand how these things support the development of the child?

๑ Are you ready for a progressive and revolutionary shift in the care and understanding of our youngest and most vulnerable fellow beings?

Rudolf Steiner did not give us a curriculum to follow. He gave us a deep and abiding picture of the human being and a breadth of understanding that included not only the fundamentals of holistic development but also the delightful summons to find joy at the foundation of our work.

Coming to terms with the depth of responsibility we recognize in our care of young children need not burden us. Rather, let us be filled with the flame of enthusiasm, knowing that we have lifetimes of learning and teams of caring partners in *high places!* We can trust that as long as we are striving toward goodness, beauty and truth, and loving the children in our care, there is forgiveness for our shortcomings and intense interest in our budding capacities.

Here is a verse to tuck into the chambers of your heart. Herbert Hahn, one of the first Waldorf teachers, wrote in *From the Wellsprings of the Soul*:

> *Remember daily that you are continuing the work*
> *of the spiritual world with the children.*
> *You are the preparers of the path for these young souls,*
> *who wish to form their lives in these difficult times.*
> *The spiritual world will always stand by you in this task.*
> *This is the wellspring of strength which you so need.*

About LifeWays North America

When one thinks about *revolution* in this 21st century, childcare and parenting may not be among the first things that come to mind. However, they are two of the most powerful areas of work with the potential to affect real change in the world. Early life experiences set the biographical stage for how much time and effort a person will need to spend overcoming those experiences, or how much strength and flexibility will be available for positive engagement with the world. What happens in the daily life environment of parents and professional childcare providers equally affects quality of life in the home and longevity of career in early childhood programs.

While on sabbatical in 1996, I was asked by a friend and business entrepreneur in Great Britain to investigate what was happening in childcare programs at the time and to consider developing an alternative approach based on healthy principles and sustainable practices. After visiting numerous "Five-Star" child-care centers and observing the overwhelm and stress exhibited by many of the children and caregivers, a group of Waldorf early childhood colleagues and I set out to try something different. Inspired by Awhina Day Nursery and Kindergarten in New Zealand and Nøkken Kindergarten in Denmark, we opened the first experimental LifeWays center in Wisconsin in 1998, along with a series of courses to explore the principles and practices that would be used in the center. The resulting LifeWays

Early Childhood Training and Certification program has been taken by nearly five hundred people, and many graduates have gone on to offer care and support based on these ideals to children birth to six and their families.

LifeWays North America provides early childhood certification programs throughout North America for childcare providers in homes and centers, home-based preschool teachers, parents, nannies, parent educators, aftercare providers and assistants in early childhood programs. These certification programs meet part-time, over the course of a year, with guided study and work with a mentor between the sessions. They fulfill the suggested guidelines for the training of childcare providers listed on the International Association of Steiner/Waldorf Early Childhood Education website. LifeWays also offers practical, hands-on workshops and seminars to support and strengthen the growing child and family. Consultation in person, by telephone or by e-mail regarding early childhood programs or parenting is also available, as well as guidance and certification for LifeWays Representative sites.

This innovative relationship-based vision for childcare, both by parents in the home and by professional childcare providers, is ideal for the healthy development of the child, as confirmed by current neurological research on the importance of bonding. LifeWays principles and suggested practices are inspired by the works of Rudolf Steiner and the experience of Waldorf education, as well as common sense and the wisdom of many generations of parents. Further information about LifeWays North America's services and sites is available at www.lifewaysnorthamerica.org; for further information about Waldorf early childhood education worldwide, please see www.iaswece.org.

Sources

- *Understanding Young Children, Excerpts from Lectures by Rudolf Steiner* is available from the Waldorf Early Childhood Association of North America, www.waldorfearlychildhood.org.

- *Home Away from Home: LifeWays Care of Children and Families* by Cynthia Aldinger and Mary O'Connell is available from LifeWays North America, www.lifewaysnorthamerica.org.

- Other books cited are available from www.steinerbooks.org and www.steinercollege.edu.store.

- Some titles are available electronically for free from the Online Waldorf Library, www.waldorflibrary.org.

About the Author

Cynthia Aldinger is founder and Executive Director of LifeWays North America. Co-author of the book *Home Away from Home: LifeWays Care of Children and Families,* Cynthia has lectured and presented internationally, directs trainings and seminars across North America, and is an Adjunct Faculty member at Rudolf Steiner College in California. She served fourteen years on the board of the Waldorf Early Childhood Association of North America and was a Waldorf Kindergarten teacher for many years after she received her Waldorf teaching certificate at Emerson College in Sussex, England. A mother and grandmother, Cynthia's passion is the preservation of the playful spirit of childhood and helping to create early childhood environments that provide the comfort, security and activities found in a healthy home.

Made in the USA
San Bernardino, CA
09 July 2015